THE SAVVY
SENIOR

THE SAVVY SENIOR

The Ultimate Guide to Health, Family, and Finances for Senior Citizens

— JIM MILLER —

HYPERION

NEW YORK

Library of Congress Cataloging-in-Publication Data

Miller, Jim
  The savvy senior: the ultimate guide to health, family, and finances for senior citizens / by Jim Miller.
     p. cm.
   ISBN 1-4013-0749-3
     1. Aged—United States. 2. Aged—Services for—United States. 3. Aged—Health and hygiene—United States. 4. Aged—United States—Family relationships. 5. Aged—Finance, Personal. I. Title.

HQ1064.U5.M54 2004
305.26′0973—dc22   2003056964

FIRST EDITION

10   9   8   7   6   5   4   3   2   1

I DEDICATE THIS BOOK TO MY PARENTS,

Joe and Joan Miller

CONTENTS

—Home—

—Health—

—Medicare and More—

—Social Security—

—Finances—

ACKNOWLEDGMENTS

I am very grateful to the many people and organizations who helped make this book possible. I would especially like to thank Susan Grossman, who helped and supported me through this process; my brother, Bob Miller; Andy Ostmeyer; Dr. Richard Mathewson; Bill Adler, with Bill Adler Books; and Mary Ellen O'Neill, my editor at Hyperion.

INTRODUCTION

MOST PEOPLE DON'T EVER THINK ABOUT SENIOR ISSUES UNTIL THEY'RE staring them in the face. Let's face it. Social Security, Medicare, hardening of the arteries and assisted-living centers aren't the most pleasant subjects for party conversations. Yet wouldn't it be nice to have a seniors' resource guide to help you cut through the maze of information overload and give you the answers and resources you're looking for?

My goal for *The Savvy Senior* is to do just that: provide senior citizens and the families who support them access to information and resources in one, easy-to-read book. The topics covered in *The Savvy Senior* are based on the thousands of questions the "Savvy Senior" newspaper column receives. In this book you will learn about the many different programs, services and discounts available to senior citizens as well as the need-to-know basics of Medicare, Social Security, estate and retirement planning, senior health issues, caregiving, grandparenting, senior housing options and much more.

People often ask me, What does an MTV-generation guy know about senior issues? Well, to that I say, I didn't know much in the beginning, but I know plenty now! I didn't start out to be a columnist or an author. In October 2000, my parents died within three weeks of each other. Feeling devastated and lost, I took a temporary job working at a retirement community to help me work through the grief. I thought being around people my parents' age would make me feel better. While I was there, I started writing a question/answer information column for senior citizens in the local newspaper, and the response was immediate. That's when it hit me; senior citizens and their families need help. Thus, the "Savvy Senior" was born and is now published in over 400 newspapers nationwide and offers an interactive Web site, along with *The Savvy Senior* book.

I hope you find *The Savvy Senior* a useful resource that is fun to read and easy to understand. But most of all, my hope is that all this information will help you become a savvy senior too.

THE SAVVY
SENIOR

LIFESTYLE

DID YOU KNOW THAT IN THE UNITED STATES TODAY, SOMEONE TURNS 50 every seven seconds, and over the next 25 years, the senior population in America (age 65 and older) will double from 35 million to over 70 million? So, it looks like you'll have plenty of company!

The Lifestyle section of *The Savvy Senior* explores some of the many options open to you as you move toward your retirement years, as well as provides valuable information if you are already there. We've tackled everything from working and volunteering to grandparenting and genealogy. Other savvy chapters will focus on topics such as senior money-saving services, senior driving and transportation, technology, fraud, and much more.

—Driver Safety Program—

Research shows a direct link between elder driving problems and senior slippage! The loss of vision, hearing, mobility and strength is usually so gradual people don't recognize it until they're faced with a sudden driving situation that they can't react to any longer. If this is you or someone you know, you need to know about the AARP Driver Safety Program. It's the nation's first and largest classroom driver improvement course specially designed for motorists age 50 and older.

 SAVVY NOTE: Since 1979, over 7.5 million people have completed this course.

The AARP Driver Safety Program administers an eight-hour course in two four-hour sessions spanning two days. The course costs $10 and helps drivers refine existing skills and develop safe, defensive driving techniques. AARP members and nonmembers alike may take the course. There are no tests.

The Driver Safety course covers the following topics:

- Vision and hearing changes
- Effects of medication
- Reaction-time changes
- Left turns and other right-of-way situations
- New laws and how they affect you
- Hazardous driving situations

 SAVVY DISCOUNTS

Upon successfully completing the eight-hour AARP Driver Safety Program course, graduates may be eligible to receive a state-mandated multiyear discount on their auto insurance premiums. Depending on the state where you live and your insurance company's policies, you may be eligible for an automobile insurance premium reduction or discount.

For more information, or to locate the AARP Driver Safety Course nearest you, call 1-888-AARP-NOW (1-888-227-7669) or log on to *www.aarp.org/55alive*.

AARP RESOURCES

- *Older Driver Skill Assessment and Resource Guide* (stock number D14957): This informative booklet includes many useful questions that help people assess their comfort with a variety of driving situations. The book also includes a number of important safety tips and reminders.
- *Community Transportation Resource Worksheet* (stock number D16686): This chart helps you make a list and keep track of what transportation options may be available in your community.

To order copies of the Guide and Worksheet, write to
AARP Fulfillment
EE 01251
601 E Street NW
Washington, DC 20049

Be sure to include the publication stock number (listed with the title) with your request.

SAVVY RESOURCES

- AAA: Many AAA-affiliated motor clubs offer an inexpensive, one-day driver improvement program for seniors. For more information, contact your local AAA office or visit the AAA Foundation for Traffic Safety's Senior Driver Web site at *www.seniordrivers.org*.
- National Safety Council: Some community groups sponsor the program Coaching the Mature Driver, a one-day class for groups of 10 or more. For more information, call 1-800-621-7619.
- National Highway Transportation Safety Administration Web site:

www.nhtsa.dot.gov. Information on safety issues, injury prevention, air bags, crash tests and much more.

- *Driving Safely While Aging Gracefully*: This booklet outlines the physical changes associated with aging, as well as tips on coping with them so that older drivers can remain safe drivers. Visit *www.nhtsa.dot.gov/people/ injury/olddrive*.
- *A Practical Guide to Alzheimer's Dementia and Driving*: Visit *www .thehartford.com/alzheimers* or write AARP Auto Insurance Program, The Hartford, Dementia and Driving Booklet, 200 Executive Blvd., Southington, CT 06489.
- The American Medical Association (AMA): Offers the physicians' guide to assessing older drivers. Log on to *www.ama-assn.org/go/olderdrivers*.
- Insurance Institute for Highway Safety: To learn what your state requires of older drivers, visit *www.hwysafety.org/safety_facts/state_laws/ older_drivers.htm*.

— Senior Transportation —

For some seniors, giving up their car is tougher than giving up their spouse! In today's world, some people think no car means no independence—but it doesn't have to. Depending on where you live, transportation options are available for most seniors.

 SAVVY NOTE: The National Institute on Aging estimates that more than 600,000 people age 70 or older stop driving each year, usually around age 85.

Transportation is the critical link that assures older Americans access to necessities such as health care and groceries. The availability of adequate transportation allows seniors the ability to live independently in their communities and helps prevent isolation. Here are some senior transportation options to look into.

Area Agencies on Aging

Your Area Agency on Aging is a great place to start. The agency provides seniors and their caregivers with specific information about community services, including transportation. The local chapters make available transportation information and contacts, as well as monitor and support specialized transportation services for seniors in their community. Contact your Area Agency on Aging for information. If you have difficulty locating your local Area Agency on Aging, call the Eldercare Locator toll free at 1-800-677-1116. The Eldercare Locator is a nationwide service to help you find information about services for older people in your own community.

The National Transit Hotline

The National Transit Hotline can provide the names of local transit providers who receive federal money to provide transportation to the elderly and people with disabilities. For more information, visit the Community Transportation Association Web site at *www.ctaa.org* and click on "Information Station," or call 1-800-527-8279.

The Yellow Pages

Let your fingers do the walking! Many telephone books have a special section in the front of the book with the names and addresses of various service organizations. Look under transportation or community services for the names of agencies that provide transportation for those with special needs.

TYPES OF TRANSPORTATION SERVICES

The type of transportation that is available in your community will vary depending upon where you live. Listed below are some possible options and contacts.

Fixed-Route Bus Transit Service

Fixed-route and scheduled services travel along an established route with designated stops where riders can board and be dropped off. Fixed-route services usually require payment of a fare on a per-ride basis.

SAVVY TIP: Many communities offer discounts to senior citizens.

Demand-Response

Also called dial-a-ride, demand-response is a system usually requiring advance reservations and offering door-to-door transportation from one specific location to another. The demand-response service provides flexibility, adapting to the needs of each rider. Demand-response service vehicles include small buses, vans and cars. This service usually requires a payment of fare or donations on a per-ride basis. Contact your Area Agency on Aging for more information. To get the number of the Agency on Aging in your area, call 1-800-677-1116.

ADA Complimentary Paratransit

The Americans with Disability Act (ADA) requires transit providers who operate a fixed-route system to also provide complimentary paratransit service. This service is for disabled or older people who are unable to use fixed-route services because of their disabilities. For more information, contact the Easter Seals Project Action at 1-800-659-6428 or visit *www.projectaction.org*.

Taxicabs

In many areas, taxis are the only form of available transportation. Though they can be expensive, taxis are a vital means of transportation for many medical patients and older persons who cannot navigate community and public transportation. Health and social service agencies sometimes provide discount taxi vouchers to low-income seniors in urban and suburban areas. Contact your local department of health and social services for more information.

Senior Centers

Community senior centers are a significant source of senior transportation. More than 15,000 senior centers across the country provide transportation to and from center activities. Many senior centers operate through the local Area Agency on Aging, but others are independent. Contact your local senior center or Area Agency on Aging for more information.

Health Care

Medicaid pays for emergency ambulance service and transportation to non-emergency medical appointments if the recipient has no other means to travel to the appointment. Medicaid-funded transportation is available in every part of the country. For more information, call your local Medicaid office or visit *www.ctaa.org/InformationStation*.

Church or Faith-Based Transportation

Many local churches or faith-based organizations offer transportation and errand services to seniors and people with disabilities. Contact your area churches for more information.

Ride Sharing

These programs coordinate people who need rides with volunteer drivers who have space in their automobiles. Typically, this service comprises scheduled transportation with specific destinations. The destination points can include places of employment, nutrition sites, senior centers and medical offices. Contact your Area Agency on Aging for more information.

—Utility Assistance—

For many seniors, money is so tight that there are months where they can't even pay their utility bills. Being able to keep the electricity and gas on is a crucial issue for seniors, especially in times of extreme hot and cold temperatures. Compounding the problem is the fact that saving on utilities requires investments in home repairs such as insulation and energy-friendly appliances, something beyond the reach of many seniors living on fixed incomes.

. . .

The good news is there are many ways for seniors to get relief when utility companies are putting on the heat to be paid. Consumer Concerns for Older Americans offers practical advice on how to prevent a utility termination before it is threatened.

Here are a few savvy options to investigate:

- **Level Payment Plans:** Customers who are current on their utility bills can establish level billing plans with utility companies. Many states require utilities to provide these plans. Your yearly bill is projected, and then divided into equal monthly installments; monthly bills reflect these amounts rather than actual per-month costs.

    Example: If your total gas bill for the year is $1,200, you would pay $100 each month instead of $200 to $300 a month in the winter and $30 to $40 a month in the summer.

- **Budget Payment Plans:** If you are so far in the red that you can't catch up, you should be able to negotiate a budget payment plan whereby you make a fixed monthly payment and the utility promises not to shut off service. If the utility pushes for a larger payment than you can afford, get help from the consumer division of your state's Public Utilities Commission.

- **Federal Energy Assistance:** The federal Low Income Home Energy Assistance Program (LIHEAP), administered by individual states, helps low-income households pay their winter heating bills. Some states also use LIHEAP funds to assist with summer cooling expenses. Guidelines for LIHEAP eligibility vary by state, but most states require that family income over the past three or twelve months be below 150 percent of the federal poverty guidelines. To apply for LIHEAP benefits, contact the local agency in your community administering the program, usually a nonprofit agency or a state welfare office, or call 1-800-674-6327.

- **Utility Fuel Funds:** Many utility companies participate in special funds to give loans or grants to those who cannot pay their utility bills. To determine the availability of these funds, contact your utility company or agency that administers the LIHEAP program. Many of these fuel funds focus specific attention on helping seniors or low-income consumers.

- **Percentage of Income Plans:** A growing number of utilities and state utilities commissions are experimenting with plans by which individuals or families pay only a certain percentage of their income instead of the amount called for by their normal utility bills. Typically, if a low-income household regularly pays this lower payment schedule, it is rewarded by gradual forgiveness of its back bills, or arrears. These plans are sometimes called Percentage of Income Plans (PIPs) or Energy Assurance Plans (EAPs), but each utility has its own unique name for its program. To find out if your utility has such a program, contact that particular utility company.

- **Discounted Rates:** Some electric, gas and water utilities have special discounted rates for low-income, elderly and/or disabled households. Ask your utility company or the state Public Utilities Commission if there is a special lower rate for seniors.

- **Energy Conservation Programs:** Some states provide homeowners and tenants with funds to weatherize their homes, thereby reducing heating and cooling costs. Many utility companies provide low-cost loans or outright grants for home weatherization, and some have sizable programs targeting seniors and/or low-income customers, providing weatherization services directly to customers. For more information, contact your local welfare office or energy department or call the Weatherization Assistance Program at 1-800-363-3732, or visit *www.eere.energy.gov/weatherization*.

SAVVY RESOURCES

- Area Agency on Aging: For the program nearest you, call the Eldercare Locator, 1-800-677-1116.
- Community Action Program (CAP): To find your local CAP program, visit the Community Action Partnership at *www.communityactionpartnership.com* or call 1-202-265-7546.
- The American Council for an Energy-Efficient Economy: A nonprofit organization dedicated to energy saving, they offer *Consumer Guide to Home Energy Savings* and an energy/money-saving checklist. Log on to *www.aceee.org*.

- National Consumer Law Center: *www.consumerlaw.org/initiatives/ seniors_initiative/lossutil.shtml.*

—Volunteerism—

Looking for something more satisfying to do with your retirement time? Ever considered volunteering? Volunteerism is a great idea for social involvement as well as making a positive contribution to your community. There are thousands of groups across the country offering community-service opportunities for volunteers age 50 and older with diverse backgrounds, skills and interests.

For individuals who are new to volunteering or who are seeking new opportunities, the **Volunteer Match** Web site is a great place to start. If you have access to the Internet, enter your ZIP code on the *www.volunteermatch.org* Web site. Local opportunities are posted by nonprofit and tax-exempt organizations. Working with thousands of local nonprofits, Volunteer Match has become the Web's largest database of volunteer opportunities.

Another great community volunteer source is the **Senior Corps**. For more than 30 years, the Senior Corps has linked over half a million older Americans to volunteer opportunities in their communities. Its three main programs include the Foster Grandparent Program, Retired and Senior Volunteer Program (RSVP) and Senior Companion Program. Each are great vehicles for interested older Americans to find challenging, rewarding and significant service right in their own backyards.

Here is a closer look at the three programs:

- **The Foster Grandparent Program** offers limited-income seniors age 60 and older opportunities to serve as mentors, tutors and loving caregivers for children and youth with special needs. They serve 20 hours a week in community organizations such as schools, hospitals, Head Start and youth centers. This program offers a small tax-free stipend, reimbursement for transportation, meals during service, annual physical examinations and accident and liability insurance while on duty.

- **The Retired and Senior Volunteer Program (RSVP)** helps people 55 and older find worthwhile service opportunities in their communities. RSVP involves seniors in service that matches their personal interests and makes use of their skills and life experiences to address priority needs in over 1,500 counties across the nation. RSVP volunteers provide hundreds of services in public and nonprofit organizations that range from education centers to police departments to hospitals. Volunteers serve from a few to over 40 hours a week.

- **The Senior Companion Program** (SCP) is part of the Senior Corps, a network of national service programs that provide older Americans with the opportunity to apply their life experiences to meeting community needs. Senior Companions serve one-on-one with the frail elderly and other homebound persons who have difficulty completing everyday tasks. They assist with grocery shopping, bill paying and transportation to medical appointments, and they alert doctors and family members to potential problems. Senior Companions also provide short periods of relief to primary caregivers. The Senior Companion Program is open to healthy individuals age 60 and over with limited incomes. This program offers a small, tax-free stipend and asks that you serve 20 hours a week.

For more information on Senior Corps programs and volunteer opportunities, call 1-800-424-8867 or see their Web site at *www.seniorcorps.org*.

Other Volunteer Resources

- **American Hospice Foundation** represents hospices that train volunteers for patient care, administrative duties and other services. For hospices near you, look in your local telephone book or go to *www.americanhospice.org*.

- **America's Second Harvest**, the nation's largest domestic hunger-relief organization, feeds hungry people by soliciting and distributing food and other grocery products through food banks and rescue programs. To find the nearest affiliate, go to *www.secondharvest.org*.

- **Big Brothers Big Sisters of America** is the country's oldest and largest youth mentoring organization, serving more than 200,000 children and youth annually in all 50 states. To contact Big Brothers Big Sisters, call 1-866-276-2447 or go to *www.bbbsa.org*.

- **Elderhostel Services Program** offers short-term volunteer projects worldwide for seniors age 55 and older. Call 1-877-426-8056 or visit *www.elderhostel.org*.

- **Global Volunteers** allows you to choose a volunteer vacation abroad or assist a USA volunteer program. Live and work with local people on life-affirming community development projects for one, two or three weeks. More than 150 service teams support some 90 host communities on five continents year-round. Call 1-800-487-1074 or log on to *www.globalvolunteers.org*.

- **Habitat for Humanity** is dedicated to eliminating poverty housing. To find an affiliate near you, check your local telephone book or go to *www.habitat.org*.

- **Meals on Wheels** depends on volunteers to deliver nutritious meals and to maintain social contact with older persons who are homebound. To locate the nearest program, go to *www.mowaa.org* and click on "Search for a Program."

- **National Mentoring Partnership** is a resource for people interested in becoming mentors to young people. For information on mentoring and local mentoring programs, go to *www.mentoring.org* or call toll free 1-888-432-6368.

- **Points of Light Foundation** mobilizes volunteers to work in communities through a network of 500 volunteer centers nationwide. Call 1-800-865-8683 or go to *www.pointsoflight.org*.

- **Rebuilding Together** is the nation's largest volunteer organization preserving and revitalizing low-income housing and communities. For more information, call 1-800-473-4229 or go to *www.rebuildingtogether.com*.

- **Volunteer America** connects individuals, families and groups with volunteer opportunities and volunteer vacations on public lands all across America. Visit *www.volunteeramerica.net*.

AARP RESOURCES

If you are a member of AARP, visit their community-service programs for volunteer opportunities, including

- The AARP Driver Safety Program, which provides a driver refresher course designed for those 50 years of age and older.
- The AARP Tax-Aide Program, which helps middle- and lower-income taxpayers—especially those 60 years of age and older—prepare their tax returns.
- The AARP Grief and Loss Program, which helps adults and their families cope with the loss of a loved one.

These programs affect communities in meaningful ways. Training is provided. For more information, contact your local AARP chapter or see their Web site at *www .aarp.org*.

—Senior Employment—

Lots of seniors are out looking for part-time employment to help supplement their Social Security. If this includes you, put your experience to work and call Experience Works, the nation's leading provider of community-service training and employment opportunities for both older and disadvantaged workers.

Established in 1965, Experience Works is a national, nonprofit organization that offers training, employment and community service opportunities for mature workers. This includes a variety of programs designed to help mature individuals enter the workforce, secure more challenging positions, move into new career areas or supplement their incomes.

Experience Works

- Serves more than 125,000 people each year
- Has more than 500 employees and offices in 44 states and Puerto Rico
- Is the largest grantee of the federal government's Senior Community Service Employment Program (SCSEP), which benefited nearly 30,000 seniors last year
- Receives funding from more than 75 public and private sources
- Operates a total budget of more than $120 million

Experience Works participants make contributions to their communities in roles as varied as teachers' aides, computer operators, emergency dispatchers, child-care providers and librarians. Many are enrolled in Experience Works training programs that teach skills required to compete in high-demand occupations, including computer technology and health care. Others, with Experience Works' help and encouragement, are pursuing high-school degrees, vocational certificates or the lifelong goal of a college education.

Experience Works Services

- **Senior Community Service Employment Program (SCSEP),** funded under Title V of the Older Americans Act, operates in 44 states. This program enables many low-income older Americans to stay off public assistance and remain productive and independent.
- **Experience Works Staffing Services** is a nationwide older-worker staffing initiative. This program provides flexible temporary, temporary-to-permanent and permanent full- and part-time employment opportunities for mature workers regardless of their age and income.
- **Experience Works Training Services** offers a wide variety of computer-skills and technology-training services and other job-related training programs.

For information on Experience Works, call 1-866-397-9757 or visit *www .experienceworks.org.*

Senior Employment Resources

- **Area Aging Agency**: a savvy resource for working options in your community. Call the Eldercare Locator at 1-800-677-1117 to find your local Aging Agency.

- **The Senior Job Bank**: Their Web site offers an easy, effective and free method for senior citizens to find occasional, part-time, flexible, temporary and even full-time jobs. Through the Senior Job Bank Web site, homeowners and businesses deal directly with older, more mature, more experienced and more reliable workers. Visit *www.seniorjobbank.org*.

- **Senior Community Service Employment Program**: *wdsc.doleta.gov/seniors*.

- **Senior Environmental Employment (SEE) Program**: *www.epa.gov/ohros/see/brochure*.

- **Senior Service America**: *www.seniorserviceamerica.org*.

- **AARP Working Options**: *www.aarp.org/working_options*.

- **Not Yet Retired**: a job-seeking site for seniors at *www.notyetretired.com*.

— Telemarketing Fraud —

Telemarketing fraud is a huge problem in America, and seniors are the number one target for this criminal activity. This kind of criminal holds you up in your own home, but not with a gun. They use a telephone!

Tele-Fraud Facts

There are approximately 140,000 telemarketing firms operating in the United States today, and it is estimated that up to 10 percent, or 14,000, may be fraudulent. The U.S. Department of Justice estimates that one out of six consumers is cheated by telemarketing criminals every year. In one case, the FBI found that fraudulent telemarketers were directing nearly 80 percent of their calls to older consumers.

SAVVY FACT: Congress estimates that telemarketing crime costs American consumers more than $40 billion. That's enough to pay for the nursing-home care of more than one million older Americans for an entire year.

Many older people preyed upon by dishonest telemarketing companies are well educated, have above-average incomes and are socially active in their communities. Therefore, the sales pitches these crooked companies use are appropriately sophisticated. Some of the most common criminal scams include phony prizes, illegal sweepstakes, sham investments, crooked charities and "recovery rooms," where victims are scammed again by telemarketers with promises that, for a fee, they will help the victims recover the money they have lost.

Beware These Common Lines You Might Hear from a Criminal Caller:

- "You are the guaranteed winner of one of three valuable prizes . . . All you need to do is pay a fee."
- "You have won a fantastic prize . . . and all you have to do is buy our vitamins."
- "Donate to charity and win a spectacular vacation."
- "Magazines at fantastic, low prices . . . I can process you now if you give me your bank account number."
- "We'll help you get back money scammed from you . . . All we need is a small fee to cover the cost."
- "Invest in a no-risk opportunity of a lifetime . . . but you need to do it today. I'll send a courier to pick up your money."

Tips to Help You Combat the Criminal Caller:

- Be wary of anyone who asks you to send money or buy anything sight unseen, unless you are certain you are dealing with a reputable firm.
- Never give out your credit card information over the phone.

- Don't pay for a free prize. Free is free. If a caller tells you the payment is for taxes on the prize, he or she has violated federal law.
- Refuse to be rushed into anything. The more a caller tries to hurry you into buying something or sending money, the more likely he or she has criminal intent.
- Offering to send a messenger to pick up your payment is a clear sign of fraudulent activity.
- Asking the caller to put the offer in writing rarely offers protection to the consumer. It often leads to credible-looking letters that in the consumer's mind seem to legitimize what in fact is a bad deal.

If you receive a suspicious call or an unsolicited one that sounds like a criminal scam, call the Fraud Hotline at 1-800-876-7060. They are open 9 A.M.–5 P.M. Eastern time, Monday–Friday. Or call your state attorney general or your local consumer protection agency.

SAVVY RESOURCES

For more information about telemarketing fraud, visit

- The National Fraud Information Center: your source for Internet and telemarketing fraud information at *www.fraud.org*.
- National Do Not Call Registry: This registry makes it easier and more efficient for you to stop getting telemarketing sales calls you don't want. Visit *www.donotcall.gov* or call toll-free 1-888-382-1222 (TTY 1-866-290-4236).
- AARP: Consumer protection against fraud. Log on to *www.aarp.org/ consumerprotect-frauds*.
- Federal Trade Commission: *www.ftc.gov*.
- National Fraud Information Center: *www.fraud.org*.
- U.S. Department of Justice: *www.usdoj.gov/criminal/fraud/telemarketing*.

—Identity Theft—

In today's credit-crazy world, thieves don't have to break into your home or bank to steal your money anymore. They only have to break into your identity by stealing your personal information, like your Social Security number, credit card records, checking account information and more.

Identity Theft Facts

According to the Federal Trade Commission,

- Over 27 million people have experienced identity theft in the last five years. That's one in nearly every ten people in this country.
- Ten million people were victims of this crime last year.
- Those victims last year lost $48 billion to the thieves.

 SAVVY NOTE: This is no small crime, and anyone who has gone through it knows the headaches it creates getting all the account numbers changed, contacting banks, etc.

Seniors Hit Hard

Seniors are especially vulnerable for a couple of reasons. Last year, an official with the Social Security Administration told the U.S. Senate's Special Committee on Aging: "Senior citizens are more likely than most to have significant assets—savings, investments, paid-up mortgages and federal entitlement checks." What's more, Uncle Sam uses Social Security numbers on Medicare, Medicaid and military identification cards, creating more exposure for seniors should they lose these documents.

What Can You Do?

Most identity theft starts with the theft of a wallet, purse or your even your mail, so try to keep the same kind of tight control on your personal and financial information that you keep on your actual money. And

- Don't give your identifying numbers or financial information over the telephone or even in person unless you are sure of the other person.
- Tear up all mail solicitations, bank records and other discarded documents. Buy a cheap shredder or just rip them up yourself.
- Call the credit reporting industry at 1-888-567-8688 to opt out of future credit card solicitations.
- Make sure your Social Security number is not on any documents that don't require it, which means in some cases taking it off checks, driver's licenses and more. It is still required on Medicare cards.
- Periodically request a copy of your credit report and review it thoroughly for errors. You can get a copy from each of the three major credit reporting agencies: Equifax 1-800-685-1111, Experian 1-888-397-3742 or Trans Union 1-800-916-8800.

If You Think You're a Victim

If you think you're a victim of identity theft, here is what you should do:

- Call your financial institutions immediately and close accounts that have been tampered with and change your Personal ID Numbers.
- Contact the fraud departments of each of the three major credit bureaus and tell them to flag your file with fraud alert: Equifax 1-800-685-1111, Experian 1-888-397-3742 or Trans Union 1-800-916-8800.
- Report it to the Federal Trade Commission Identity Theft Hotline at 1-877-IDTHEFT (1-877-438-4338).
- Call your local police department to file a report.

SAVVY RESOURCES

- Identity Theft Resource Center: a nationwide nonprofit organization that fights identity theft by supporting victims, broadening public awareness, disseminating information about this crime and decreasing the potential victim population. Visit *www.idtheftcenter.org*.

- Federal Trade Commission: your national resource for identity theft, at *www.consumer.gov/idtheft*.
- 101 Identity Theft: This Web site contains lots of news and information on what to do if identity theft happens to you. Visit *www.101-identitytheft.com*.

—Visiting Grandchildren—

Does a visit from your grandchildren stress you out? If so, you're not alone! Here are a few pointers to help ease your nerves and make for a more enjoyable visit.

Before the Visit

To help avoid some possible bumps in the road, talk to your son or daughter about their rules and routines before the visit. For example, How much television can they watch? When is bed- or naptime? What do they like to eat? How do you handle fighting or behavior issues? Are they allergic to anything? Learning some of the basics beforehand can help pave the way for a smoother visit. Also, set some ground rules and stick to them. Remember, when grandkids are disciplined to obey your rules, everyone enjoys their visit more. Including you!

 SAVVY TIP: The number one thing that most grandparents do before grandkids visit is buy snack food. Just be sure it's of the healthy variety and not loaded with sugar.

What to Do?

The best thing to do with your grandchildren is give them your attention and try to meet them on their level. It's the little things that matter, so don't worry if you don't have a computer or video games to keep them occupied. If you do, great! Otherwise, here are a few shared activities to consider:

- Exercising or sports
- Cooking and eating
- Shopping
- Watching television or videos
- Gardening or yard work
- Board games or cards
- Arts and crafts
- Park, zoo, swimming, fishing or picnicking
- Movie theater
- Public library

These activities, along with your kind attention, are a winning combination!

Safety Considerations

Here are some home safety tips for visits by young grandchildren:

- Childproof your house by moving valuable or breakable items out of reach of little hands. Older kids can also be rambunctious, so be prepared.
- Move cleaning products and other poisons out of low cabinets. Keep medicine in a locked cabinet.
- Block electrical outlets with plugs and be careful of electrical cords.
- Have medical information and emergency phone numbers handy just in case.

Bottom Line

This time with your grandchildren is a special time. Use this golden opportunity to listen to them, talk to them, ask questions and show your affection. Make memories together that you and your grandchildren will cherish for years to come!

SAVVY RESOURCES

- AARP: Find information on discipline, safety, traveling with grandchildren, history sharing and having a successful visit at *www.aarp.org/grandparents*.

- Cyber Parent: Lists activities divided by age group and provides grandparenting information at *www.cyberparent.com/gran*.
- Yahooligans: This Web guide for children offers kid-friendly links to sites about games, crafts, science, sports and jokes at *www.yahooligans.com*.

— Grandparenting from Afar —

Distance doesn't necessarily make the heart grow fonder. Sometimes it makes you forget, which is a concern for many grandparents living far away from their grandchildren. While there is no substitute for actually being there, there are some things you can do to play an important and active role in their lives. Here are a few savvy tips to help you stay connected.

Visual Connection

- Send recent photos of yourselves to your grandchildren and ask your children to place them at a height where a small child can see them.
- Videotape yourself reading stories or singing songs so the children can see you and hear your voice whenever they like.
- If both households have home computers with Internet access, get a Web video camera and microphone and talk over the Internet anytime for free.

Visits

- Determine whether it is more practical for you to visit your children or for them to visit you.
- Include a visit on your way to or from somewhere else.
- Try phone or e-mail visits. Set up a time each month or week to call, or exchange e-mail and have online chats.

Vacationing Together

- Ask what subjects your grandchildren are studying in school. Plan a trip to see some of the places they may have heard about or studied.
- Do they know where you were born? Show them the town where you grew up.
- Spend time taking pictures while on vacation. Build a scrapbook together, including postcards and souvenirs from the places you visit.

Keeping in Touch

- Try to connect with your grandchildren on a regular basis via telephone or e-mail.
- Ask questions about their activities and follow up on their interests.
- Keep a list of each grandchild's important dates, such as birthday, school events, holidays and other milestones. For major events, send a few notes or even little gifts several times before the date.
- Be consistent. Don't promise what you can't deliver.

Activities

- Playing games together can be an enjoyable pastime. Ask your grandchildren about their favorite games and if they can teach them to you. Or teach them a game you enjoy.
- Learn about their favorite sports so you can talk with them about their games, their successes and difficulties.
- Read together. By reading the same books or stories, you can engage them in further conversation. And they will be thrilled that you like the same things.

- The Foundation for Grandparenting: *www.grandparenting.org*
- Grandparents' Web: *www.cyberparent.com/gran*
- AARP for grandparents: *www.aarp.org/grandparents*

—Financial Tips for Grandparents Raising Grandchildren—

If you're a grandparent raising your grandchild, you're not alone! Did you know that 4.5 million children in the United States under age 18 are growing up in grandparent-headed households? That's a 30 percent increase since 1990.

Financial Help

Grandparents often have limited or fixed incomes on which to live and provide financial support for their grandchildren. Here are some possible state-funded financial assistance options to look into:

- **Subsidized Guardianship:** Some states offer monthly payments to relatives who become the legal guardians of children in their care. Each state has its own criteria a relative must meet before one can participate in the program. Contact your state or regional office of the Administration for Children and Families for more information.
- **Adoption Assistance:** Both federal and state programs can offer help to adoptive parents. These programs provide a monthly subsidy for the child. The adopting parents (who may be grandparents) do not have to meet any financial eligibility criteria to receive adoption assistance on behalf of the child. In addition, federal legislation makes medical assistance, payment of legal fees and nonrecurring expenses available to adoptive parents. For more information,

contact your state or regional office of the Administration for Children and Families.

- **Temporary Assistance for Needy Families:** TANF offers financial help to families with low incomes. Specific rules mandate that work requirements be met if a caregiver requests financial assistance for himself/herself and the child. However, state policies vary in this area (as well as with the type of grant you receive), so you need to check with your state or regional office of the Administration for Children and Families.

Tax Breaks

The Savvy Senior has also found that grandparents raising grandchildren may be eligible to pay lower taxes. If you are a grandparent who had income from work and can claim a "qualifying child," you may qualify for any or all of these:

- **The Earned Income Tax Credit (EITC):** This option can provide tax credits to workers who are raising children, thereby reducing or eliminating federal income taxes. Some low-income workers actually get money from the government—a "negative income tax." You must, however, meet income requirements, which vary depending on how many children you are raising, and you must file a federal tax return. Eligible employed grandparents can file a W-5 form with their employer and receive advance payments during the year that increase the amount of money taken home in each paycheck. Check with your employer to get this form.

SAVVY NOTE: Of the 43 states (plus the District of Columbia) that have personal income taxes, 11 now have state EITCs: Colorado, Iowa, Kansas, Maryland, Massachusetts, Minnesota, New York, Oregon, Rhode Island, Vermont and Wisconsin. In these states, contact your state department of revenue to learn if you are eligible and how to apply.

- **The Child and Dependent Care Credit:** This credit option helps families who must pay for child care in order to work or look for work. This credit reduces federal income tax. Unlike the EITC, it does not provide refunds to families who do not pay federal income tax. The dollar amount of the credit depends on the number of children, family income and the amount paid for care. For more information, call your local IRS office or the national office at 1-800-829-1040 or visit *www.irs.gov*.

- **The Child Tax Credit:** This third credit option can also be claimed on your federal income tax. This credit reduces the federal income tax but, like the Child and Dependent Care Credit, does not provide refunds over the amount of income tax paid. A family making too much money to receive the Earned Income Tax Credit may still qualify for a Child Tax Credit. The "qualifying child" must be under age 17, a U.S. citizen or resident alien, and must have been claimed as a dependent on the previous year's federal income tax return. Grandchildren are identified as qualified dependents. For more information, call your local IRS office or the national office at 1-800-829-1040 or visit *www.irs.gov*.

SAVVY NOTE: Grandparents can be eligible for both the Earned Income Credit and the Child Tax Credit. Be sure to ask about the "Additional Child Tax Credit" if you are raising three or more dependent children. Under certain circumstances, where federal income tax is less than the maximum Child Tax Credit and payroll taxes (Social Security and Medicare) are greater than any EITC benefit, working grandparents raising grandchildren may be eligible for the "Additional Child Tax Credit."

SAVVY RESOURCES

- The AARP Grandparent Information Center (GIC): This resource provides information about services and programs that can help improve the lives of grandparent-headed households. Phone 1-202-434-2296 or visit *www.aarp.org/grandparents*.
- Grand Parent Again: This Web site offers information about education, legal support, support groups and other organizations for grandparents raising grandchildren. Visit *www.grandparentagain.com*.
- The Child Welfare League of America: CWLA is an association of more than a thousand public and nonprofit agencies that directly help more than

three million at-risk children and youth and their families. Log on at *www.cwla.org*.

- Generations United: the premier national organization focusing solely on promoting intergenerational strategies, programs and policies. This site has several fact sheets about grandparents and other relatives raising grandchildren: *www.gu.org/projg&o.htm*.
- Children's Defense Fund: CDF provides a voice for all children in America. Their Web site provides information about Kinship Care and initiatives across the nation: *www.childrensdefense.org*.
- Childhelp USA: This group focuses on treatment, prevention and research, and operates the National Child Abuse Hotline at 1-800-422-4453, staffed 24 hours a day, seven days a week. Also see *www.childhelpusa.org*.

— Money-Managing Grandparents —

Teaching your grandchildren the practice of good money management is a beautiful gift and gives them a head start on the road to financial stability. Who knows, you might even learn something yourself! Here are some savvy tips to consider.

How to Start

The best way is teaching by example. The way you handle your own finances can show your grandchildren that you value handling money properly. Talk with them about how you use a budget, how you decide to spend money and how you make choices. You might, for example, help them understand how to set limits on spending by deciding between getting either two movies or video games from the video rental store or just one movie and lunch at their favorite restaurant.

You can also use your own experiences to make it clear to grandchildren that when you write a check, use a debit card or withdraw from an ATM, you are spending money you have previously deposited in the bank. They can learn that these modern tools are the same as paying with cash and not magic, bottomless sources of money.

Develop Saving Habits

Experience is often the best teacher, and you can help your grandchildren in various ways to experience handling money. First, of course, they must have some money if they are to learn to manage it.

Teach Them about Getting Money

Your grandchildren may have an allowance from parents or you may provide one. If you are giving them an allowance, make sure that "pay day" is a regular occurrence. Offer grandchildren the opportunity to earn extra money, not for regular responsibilities but for extras like yard work or washing the car.

Teach Them about Saving Money

Your grandchildren should set a savings goal—how much they want to save and what they'd like to save for. For younger grandchildren, a photograph or magazine picture of what they are saving for can help reinforce the goal. Older grandchildren can grasp the concept of longer-term goals, like that first car or a college education. Delaying gratification is hard for children to do, but you can help them practice this skill.

Help Them Open a Savings Account

This could be at a bank, but you can also use a piggy bank or even an old coffee can, depending on the age of your grandchildren. Show them how to keep track of their money either through the bank passbook or with a special notebook for recording and adding up the money they are saving. An added bonus here is the practical application of their math skills. If you are using a bank savings account, older grandchildren can learn important financial terms like *deposit*, *withdrawal* and *interest*.

Contributing to Your Grandchildren's Savings

There are many ways grandparents can help their grandchildren's savings grow. You may want to consider actually adding money to their savings by

- Matching the dollar amount each grandchild puts in a savings account—similar to an employer matching an employee's contributions to a 401(k) plan,
- Giving cash or savings bonds as gifts, or
- Opening an IRA or Education Fund.

SAVVY RESOURCES

- Kiplinger: offers great information about kids and money, and answers to questions kids frequently ask: *www.kiplinger.com.*
- The American Savings Education Council (ASEC): offers savings tools for children, including an interactive Savings Calculator: *www.asec.org.*

—The 529 Plan—

SAVING FOR YOUR GRANDCHILDREN'S COLLEGE EDUCATION

Helping to save for your grandchildren's college educations is like saving for retirement. Time, not timing, is the key! And a savvy tool to help you save is the 529 plan. Here's what you should know.

Cost Increases

A grandchild born in 2004 and enrolling in college 18 years from now will face huge expenses. In the last couple of years, many colleges have seen costs climb by more than 20 percent. Nationwide, the average is closer to 10 percent the last two years. But, being optimistic and using an inflation rate of 5 percent, a public university that now charges $9,000 a year for tuition, fees, books and room and board will cost nearly $90,000 for four years when it comes time for that newborn to enroll there. And that $9,000 estimate is on the low end of college costs today.

The sad truth is that many middle-class and even upper-middle-class parents won't be able to save the kind of money it will take to pay for college 18 years from now, nor will children and grandchildren be able to work their way through school. They are going to need some help, and the 529 plan is a great option.

529 Facts

A 529 plan is a state-sponsored college savings plan that helps families save for future college costs. Available in every state, 529 plans can help grandparents like yourself contribute to their grandchildren's college education in an easy, tax-free way. Here are some of the advantages:

- You get unsurpassed tax breaks for contributions. Your investment grows tax-free as long as your money stays in the 529 plan. And when you withdraw money from your plan to pay for college, the money is federally tax-free as well.
- You the donor stay in control of the account. With few exceptions, the named beneficiary has no rights to the funds. In other words, you don't need to worry that your 18-year-old granddaughter will cash in her college fund and run off to Mexico to marry some kid in a rock band. You call the shots!
- The 529 is easy! Once you decide which 529 plan to use, you complete a simple enrollment form and make your contributions or sign up for automatic deposits.
- Everyone is eligible to take advantage of a 529 plan. Generally, there are no income restrictions or age limitations.
- Many states also offer multiple 529 investment options, from high risk to conservative, and as the child ages, the money can be moved to more conservative funds for safekeeping.
- Just because you save money under a specific state's program doesn't mean the beneficiary of the account is necessarily required to go to school in that state. Check with your state to make sure there are no limits.
- If your grandchild doesn't go to college, you'll have to pay a 10 percent penalty on the earnings. Which means that you will get back 100 percent of your principal and 90 percent of your earnings.

SAVVY RESOURCES

For complete information on state-sponsored 529 plans, see these Web sites.

- Saving for College: A comprehensive Web site offering valuable information on the 529 plans. Visit *www.savingforcollege.com* or call 1-800-400-9113.
- The College Savings Plans Network: Intended to make higher education more attainable, the Network serves as a clearinghouse for information among existing college savings programs. Visit *www.collegesavings.org* or call 1-877-277-6496.

—Traveling with Your Grandchildren—

How about a road trip with the grandkids? If you would like to treat your grandkids to a travel outing but have some reservations, read on!

Traveling with someone two generations behind you can definitely create some challenging moments, but if you practice flexibility, you will greatly increase your chances of a smooth journey. Here are a few savvy tips for traveling with your grandchildren that can help you maintain a balance of excitement, rest, learning and fun.

Where to Go and What to Do

Children are more interested in activity than information. They learn through active involvement. Take them to places that will make an impression, either because of what they actively do there or because of something unique about the setting. You also might consider taking a volunteer vacation, where you and your grandchildren can share a learning experience while providing community service.

Things to Consider

- Don't plan every minute—things will invariably take longer than anticipated. Allow time for spontaneous activities the children are interested in.
- Intersperse high levels of physical activity with more quiet times. Children build up energy and will need opportunities to "burn it off" by swimming, running or climbing every one to two hours.
- Invite the children to have some say about the itinerary. Be flexible.
- Familiarize yourself with the safety needs and capabilities of your grandchildren.
- Balance special attractions, such as the zoo or a sporting event, with time spent doing something quiet together, like reading, taking a walk or watching a movie.
- Invite your grandchildren to bring a friend along. They will have more fun and there will be less of a drain on you to provide entertainment all the time.
- Consider inviting one or two of your friends along to help you out and allow for some "grown-up" conversation.
- Plan backup activities. Bring books, games or a personal cassette or CD player with familiar music, which can be used in the car, airplane or train, on rainy days or while waiting in lines or in restaurants.
- Pack plenty of healthy snacks for good energy levels. Children generally need to eat frequently, and behavior will be best if they have lots of water, protein and fruit rather than sugary or high-fat foods.
- Check into child and older adult discounts; successful travel with your grandchildren does not have to be an expensive proposition.

Savvy Extras

- Discuss the rules at the beginning of the trip. Let the children know what is expected of them.
- Give each child a spending allotment and be clear about any limits on what they buy.

- Be a role model for your grandchildren. Show them that learning is a lifelong undertaking. Be curious and enthusiastic about the things you learn on your trip together.
- Keep a trip journal and encourage them to do the same if they are old enough. Write down some of the funny or profound things your grandchildren say.
- Listen to their songs, laugh at their jokes or watch them play a video game. You have a special role in your grandchildren's lives, and giving them your time and attention will make a lifelong impression. The most important thing is to have fun and experience things together!

When It's Over

Every trip comes to an end. It may not have been all you hoped it would be, but the special moments you shared are what you and your grandchildren will remember. It won't matter if you forgot the suntan lotion, missed a flight, packed the wrong clothes or visited a boring museum. Schedule some time later to look over your photographs and journals, and you will all remember the times spent laughing and learning together. The savvy information that follows was obtained from AARP.

SAVVY RESOURCES

- The Foundation for Grandparenting: This nonprofit organization is dedicated to supporting grandparents. Visit *www.grandparenting.org*.
- Elderhostel Services Program offers short-term volunteer projects worldwide for seniors age 55 and older: 1-877-426-8056 or *www.elderhostel.org*.
- GRANDTRAVEL: This is a commercial vacation travel program for grandparents and grandchildren, at *www.grandtrvl.com*.
- *Unbelievably Good Deals and Great Adventures That You Absolutely Can't Get Unless You're Over 50*, by Joan Rattner Heilman. A wonderful guide to good deals and great adventures. Cost: $14.95.
- Volunteer America connects individuals, families and groups with volunteer opportunities and volunteer vacations on public lands across America. Visit *www.volunteeramerica.net*.

- Cross-Cultural Solutions is a not-for-profit international volunteer organization that offers a unique opportunity for participants to work side by side
with local people on locally designed and driven projects. Volunteer programs
operate in Brazil, China, Costa Rica, Ghana, Guatemala, India, Peru, Russia,
Tanzania and Thailand. Visit *www.crossculturalsolutions.com* or call
1-800-380-4777.

—Genealogy 101—

Did you ever wonder where you came from? No, I'm not talking about Adam and
Eve! I'm talking about genealogy, one of the most popular and fastest-growing
hobbies among boomers and seniors today. If you're interested in tracking down
your roots but don't know where to start, here are some savvy suggestions to help
you begin. Happy hunting!

- "How-to" genealogy books help you begin, and show you how to organize the
data. Check the library or a genealogical society. Cindi Howell's book *Cindi's
List*, 2nd Edition (two volumes), and *Genealogy for Dummies* are good guides.
An excellent magazine is *The Family Chronicle: The Magazine for Families
Researching Their Roots*.
- Join a local genealogical society. Check to see if there is a state historical society. These organizations often sponsor workshops for those beginning the family genealogical project. Does your local Church of Christ of the Latter-Day
Saints sponsor a Family History Center? The Family History Centers have access
to the largest genealogical library in the world, located in Salt Lake City, Utah.
- Start at home and work backward. Do not skip generations. Collect all birth
certificates, pictures, letters, photographs (be sure to put the date, place and
names on the photos), cards, newspaper clippings and funeral notices. Also

include school report cards, school diplomas and special awards that you have at home.

- Talk to your family members about grandparents, uncles and aunts. Record their birth dates, date and place of marriages. Where did they grow up? Record death certificates and cemetery locations.

 SAVVY TIP: Ask relatives if anyone else in the family is doing family genealogy research. You might be able to compare notes.

- Always write and record all information, no matter how trivial. Be organized! At the beginning, document the site and origin of your information in a genealogy research log. Who and what does the information relate to?
- Check local libraries for city directories that will list head of household, occupation, street addresses and other occupants of the residence. Old local newspapers may be available on microfilm or microfiche. Check for old high-school yearbooks. Often local cemetery lists are kept at the library. Local libraries are savvy sources of information!
- Federal census records, recorded every 10 years, date back to 1790, with the exception of 1890, when the records were destroyed by fire. Start here and work backward. Check for alternative name spellings, as names may have been misspelled. The family information varies from decade to decade. Later census forms list head of household, relatives, ages, places of birth, countries of birth of parents, plus other valuable information.
- Computers, genealogy software and the Internet are savvy sources with which to begin research, but they are not essential. *Rootsweb.com* is the place to look for links to sites on how to begin your research.

 SAVVY NOTE: Don't jump to the conclusion that you will solve all the family history problems on the Internet.

- Be patient. It is rare that a single source of records will give you all the family history. There will be days spent without success, but every so often there is one "magical moment" when a new piece of family history surfaces. Family genealogy is a time-consuming project that ultimately proves very rewarding.

BRICKWALL SOLUTIONS

Have you gotten stuck yet? If you spend much time researching your genealogy and go far enough back you're bound to, as they say in the genealogy world, hit a brick wall. But, with persistence and a few helpful resources, the missing pieces of your family puzzle can hopefully come together. Here are a few suggestions to work with.

How Do You Spell That?

Your relatives may not be where you thought they were going to be or should be. Especially in census data, names are sometimes misspelled. For example, let's say the real given name is "Smith," but in the 1880 census it was recorded as "Smyith." Be sure to check all the spelling options.

Web Sources

- Use the Internet search engines such as the Family History Library, *www.familysearch.org*, or Random Acts of Genealogical Kindness, at *www.raogk.org*. These Web sites offer assistance from local volunteers listed by state and then by county and city.
- Don't underestimate the value of message boards in the several large genealogy data base managers such as *Genealogy.com* or *Ancestry.com*.
- Search the sources located at the large number of Web sites on *rootsweb.com* and *cyndislist.com*.
- You also might want to start an Internet Web page using your father's, or mother's, name so researchers scanning for a similar name can respond. See *usgenweb.com* for more information.
- Visit *familychronicle.com* for their published histories of "Brickwall" solutions.

Dig Deeper

- State and county court records can help you clear the brick wall. The county clerk's office will have death certificates and records. The probate judge's office may have old wills, land records and other information.

- Death records outside of the courthouse may be easy to find in the local libraries. The library will have old city directories, which will list addresses of old family homes, occupants and employment.

- Many libraries have microfilmed copies of old local newspapers back to the 1800s. Marriage announcements may list the bride and groom's birth dates and their parents. Check the same paper several weeks later for a more expanded wedding announcement. Look for 25- and 50-year wedding announcements, which sometimes give couples' family histories. Most interesting are newspaper obituaries. An obituary may list the date of birth of the deceased, where they were born, their parents' names and brothers and sisters. Also, divorces in the immediate family may be listed, as well as cities and states of children, with their spouses' names. The funeral home, church and minister providing the final service will be noted. Check to see if these records may be available.

- Community histories are written about counties, townships and towns. These can be great sources of biographic information of your lost relatives. Check with your local library to see what is available.

- Search the local cemetery listed with the dates of birth and death etched in stone. Check nearby gravestones for other relatives and ancestors.

- If your search involves a male member of the family, check to see if he was a member of a Masonic Lodge. The local and state Masonic organizations keep excellent and extensive records. This would include the date the member joined the lodge, the location of the lodge, the Masonic degrees earned and the death date. Also, check the Masonic Web sites on the Internet.

- Visit antiques shops in the area. Often copies of old high-school or college yearbooks may be found with pictures of your parent or forgotten and/

or unknown relatives. There may be old church directories or local history books in the shops. Shop owners often know the local history of their area.

Keep searching! Help can come from lots of directions, and the missing piece of your puzzle might be just around the corner.

—Become a Computer-Savvy Senior—

Getting Started

There are many ways to learn basic computer and Web skills. *The Savvy Senior* recommends you begin with a basic computer skills class. Start by checking with your local public library, high school, community college, university or vo-tech for possible options. If these are not available, find a computer-savvy friend or family member to teach you.

 SAVVY TIP: If all of the above fails, call your local high school or college to see if they have any students who could come over or meet with you to get you started.

If you are the type who prefers learning on your own at your own pace, there are some computer programs that come with built-in tutorials, and there are countless books and videos available that provide resources to help you learn. Ask your librarian, bookstore or computer supply store to help you choose materials that you feel comfortable with.

 SAVVY TIP: For new computer users: People learn best by doing, so there is no substitute for practice! Put what you learn into use right away. This will reinforce what you have learned and help you retain it.

The World Wide Web

The World Wide Web is a great tool to help keep you connected to the important things in life. In fact, a recent survey indicated that the key reasons seniors enjoy the Internet is because it allows them easy access to keep in touch with family and friends, as well as keep up with news and information and even do a little shopping. Other statistics show that

- Seniors age 65 and up constitute the fastest-growing group of American Internet users.
- On a typical day, 69 percent of wired seniors use the Internet, compared with 56 percent of all users, and seniors use e-mail as much as any other age group, according to the U.S. Department of Commerce. You can too!

SAVVY RESOURCES

Here are some great resources for new senior computer users:

- SeniorNet: a nonprofit organization of computer-using adults age 50 and older. SeniorNet provides older adults education for and access to computer technologies to enhance their lives and enable them to share their knowledge and wisdom. Visit them at *www.seniornet.org*.
- CyberSeniors.org: a nonprofit organization dedicated to connecting seniors to the world at their fingertips. It provides educational opportunities for seniors to learn at little or no cost how to use computers and access the wealth of information available on the Internet. For more information, visit *www.CyberSeniors.org*.
- Learn the Net: This site has excellent do-it-yourself resources such as tutorials on e-mail, newsgroups, Web publishing, Internet research, etc. See *www.learnthenet.com*.
- *Computer Friendly*, by Raymond Steinbacher: new computer training course designed specifically for beginners. You'll learn how to navigate through Windows 95 or Windows 98, master basic desktop publishing and create your

own files and spreadsheets. You'll also learn to understand the Internet and create and send messages to people around the world. The cost is $12.95, plus shipping and handling. Call 1-814-833-6353 or visit *www.greentreepress.com*.

- Ask Mr. Modem: a great how-to resource for senior computer users. The site offers books and a newsletter: *www.mrmodem.com*.
- CNET: If you're shopping for a computer and want to compare product features as well as prices, visit *www.computers.com*.
- Free and low-cost Internet service: Visit *www.NetZerO.com* and *www.Juno.com*.
- The Purple Book: a comprehensive Internet shopping guide (with more than 1,600 entries) that informs consumers about the best online shopping opportunities available on the Web: *www.thepurplebook.com*.
- Senior Discounts.com: *www.seniordiscounts.com*.
- AARP Computers & Technology: helps you get the most out of the brave new world of technology. Visit *www.aarp.org/comptech*.

Savvy Books

- *PCs for Dummies* (8th Edition), by Dan Gookin (Wiley)
- *The Complete Idiot's Guide to PCs* (8th Edition), by Joe Kraynak (Prentice Hall)
- *The Macintosh Bible* (8th Edition), by Clifford Colby and Marty Cortinas, editor (Peachpit)
- *Macs for Dummies* (7th Edition), by David Pogue (Wiley)

HOME

HOME SWEET HOME! A RECENT AARP HOUSING SURVEY SAID THAT MOST seniors, 83 percent in fact, want to remain in their homes as long as possible. In our Home section are suggestions that will help you to do just that. *The Savvy Senior* has tips for making your home safe, as well as a list of gadgets you can use to help manage your living space, particularly if you have arthritis. If the thought of downsizing your home is overwhelming, check out the chapter on how to slowly and thoughtfully lighten your load as you transition into a smaller living environment.

Perhaps the most difficult thing for seniors and their families is knowing when it's time to decide whether to move into a retirement or assisted-care facility, and getting an understanding of the many options available. Aging parents may opt to live with their grown children, or children might try to assist their elderly parents from afar. This section covers all the issues that might come up on this subject, and explains the various senior housing options available, such as continuing-care retirement, assisted living, alternatives for senior care and nursing-home care. In addition, *The Savvy Senior* provides the resources to help you make these decisions.

—Home Modification—

Imagine the perfect senior home: no steps, wide doorways to accommodate wheelchairs, ramps, easy-to-use door levers, large cabinet knobs, nonslip floors, lowered cabinets, higher wall outlets and grab bars everywhere. Add low maintenance, inside and out, and you'd be all set! Well, that might be a little too much to ask. However, there are some simple modifications that can be done and some programs that can help you afford it.

With the rapid growth of the aging American population, home safety modification is becoming more and more common. By adding supportive features to your home, you increase your ability to move freely and safely about it. Ultimately, home modifications and repairs prevent injury and falls that can lead to expensive hospitalization and institutional living.

Home Modification Considerations

Here are a few age-proofing considerations to add to your list:

- Remove clutter and electrical cords throughout the house.
- Install grab bars in the shower, near the toilet and by the tub.
- Replace tubs with walk-in showers (nice alternative).
- Install flexible shower heads.
- Place nonskid strips or decals in the tub or shower.
- Replace hard-to-turn faucet handles and doorknobs with lever handles.
- Improve lighting.
- Put easy-to-grab ring handles on cabinets.
- Use sliding shelves.
- Widen doorways and hallways to a minimum of 35 inches.
- Lower door thresholds to one half inch or less. Transition wedges can be used if threshold is higher.
- Install handrails for support.

- Install ramps for accessible entry and exit.
- Install insulation, storm windows and air-conditioning.

 SAVVY TIP: Simple items can be purchased at your local hardware store for a minimal cost.

DISCOUNT RESOURCES

Home modification programs in your area may provide reduced rates, loans or services free of charge. Check out the following possibilities:

- Your state or local Area Agency on Aging may have funds from the Older Americans Act Title III to repair and modify homes. Call the Eldercare Locator at 1-800-677-1116 to find your local aging agency.
- Community Development Block Grants help citizens maintain and upgrade their homes. For more information call HUD at 1-202-708-1577 or visit *www.hud.gov*.
- Home equity conversion mortgages allow homeowners to turn the value of their homes into cash, without having to move or make regular loan payments; ask your local lender or bank about this option.
- Medicare and Medicaid can fund some durable medical equipment (such as grab bars and bath/shower chairs). Check with your physician or health-care provider.
- Contact your local Housing Authority for grant and/or loan programs for home-modification and repair services for seniors and adults with disabilities.
- USDA Rural Development offers 1 percent interest repair loans to very-low-income and elderly homeowners and repair grants of up to $7,500 to the elderly that qualify. Call the USDA Rural Housing Service at 1-202-720-5177 or visit *www.rurdev.usda.gov/rhs*. You can also contact the USDA Office of Communications at 1-202-690-1533 to request the field office that covers your area, or visit *www.usda.gov*.

- Two programs from the Low Income Home Energy Assistance Program and the Weatherization Assistance Program of the U.S. Department of Energy provide funds to weatherize the homes of lower-income persons. For more information, contact the Office of State and Community Programs at 1-800-363-3732 or *www.eere.energy.gov/weatherization*.
- The National Center for Seniors' Housing Research provides updated information on the latest trends, technologies and issues regarding seniors' housing. Visit *www.nahbrc.org/seniors* or call 1-800-638-8556.

This information was provided in part by the National Resource Center on Supportive Housing and Home Modification.

—Fall Prevention—

Did you know that nearly half of all falls for senior citizens occur at home? It's estimated that in the United States, one of every three people age 65 or older falls each year, and falls are the leading cause of death from injuries among the elderly. So, before it's too late, take some precautions to "fall-proof" your home and yourself.

 SAVVY NOTE: Two-thirds of seniors who fall have a repeat fall within six months.

It's good to remember that falling is not the result of just getting older. However, the older you get, the more it can hurt and cause serious and even fatal injury. Most falls occur while you're doing everyday activities at home, especially on stairs and in kitchens, bathrooms and bedrooms. Here are some preventive household tips to help you stay upright and reduce your chances of falling.

"Fall-Proof" Your Home

- Make sure there is a clear walkway through every room. It is a good idea to remove tripping hazards such as books, clothes, shoes and extension cords from walkways. Objects out of their normal place that are overlooked can cause a person to trip.
- Throw away the throw rugs or use double-sided tape to keep the rugs from slipping. Tack down the edges of all loose carpets.
- Keep items you use often in cabinets you can reach easily without using a step stool.
- Have grab bars put in next to your toilet and in the tub or shower.
- Use nonslip mats in the bathtub and on shower floors. Use nonskid mats, abrasive strips or carpet on any bathroom surface that may get wet.
- Good lighting can prevent many falls. Make sure that light switches are easy to get to and are installed at both the top and bottom of a stairway.
- Install nightlights in the bedroom, bathroom and hallways.
- Have handrails and lights put in on all staircases.
- Arrange furniture and other objects so that there are wide, clear aisles for walking.

"Fall-Proof" Yourself

- Wear shoes that give good support and have thin, nonslip soles. Avoid wearing slippers and athletic shoes with deep treads.
- Have your eyes checked! You may be wearing the wrong glasses or have a condition such as glaucoma or cataracts that limits your vision.
- Have your hearing checked! You may have some inner ear problems that affect your balance.
- Review your medications with your doctor or pharmacist. Some drugs can make you drowsy, dizzy or unsteady.
- Do you drink alcohol? Even a small amount can affect coordination and reaction time.

- Exercise! Ask your doctor to help plan an exercise program that will improve your strength, flexibility and balance.

SAVVY RESOURCES

- Centers for Disease Control and Prevention: *www.cdc.gov/ncipc/duip/spotlite/falfacts.htm*
- American Academy of Orthopedic Surgeons: *http://orthoinfo.aaos.org*
- American Academy of Otolaryngology: *www.entnet.org/healthinfo/balance/fall.cfm*
- The National Safety Council: *www.nsc.org/issues/ifalls/falfalls.htm*

—Gadgets for Seniors—

Household senior gadgets are a great way to help aging seniors maintain their independence and even improve their quality of life. Senior gadgets, also known as assistive devices, are fun, practical items that are designed to help with such activities as getting dressed, taking a shower, reaching out-of-the-way places, opening doors, reading, writing, remembering to take medications and hearing the person on the other end of the telephone line. Here is a savvy sampling of what's currently available.

Trouble Hearing

- Telephone amplifiers with adjustable tone, pitch and volume
- Flashing-light phones, doorbells and smoke-alarm adapters
- Cordless headphones for televisions and audio devices
- Vibrating alarm clocks you can place under your pillow

Trouble Seeing

- Talking watches, clocks, timers, calculators, scales and indoor/outdoor thermometers
- Talking heart, blood-pressure and blood-sugar monitors
- Tactile knobs for stoves with raised dots to indicate settings
- Battery-operated lighted magnifiers for reading
- Large-print labelers that print raised, half-inch-high letters and numbers onto sticky-backed tape
- Magnifiers for televisions and computer screens
- VideoEye power magnification system
- Voice-activated automatic telephone dialers
- Remote controls with large buttons and numbers (or voice-activated) for televisions, cable boxes and VCRs
- Computers with voice-recognition and speech software and large-letter keyboards

Trouble Remembering

- Electronic pillboxes with alarms that signal when to take medication
- Telephones with memory dialing and spaces for photos of people called frequently
- Timed faucets that automatically turn off water
- Audiocassette tapes and books with memory-improvement exercises

Trouble Getting Around and Performing Everyday Activities

- Plastic finger loops that help turn keys in doors and car ignitions
- Long-handled reaches for retrieving items on low or high shelves
- Implements that help in putting on socks or stockings
- Lever-style adapters that make it easy to turn door handles and faucets

- Writing aids such as large grips for pens, and pen designs that help reduce the shake and muscle pain of writing
- Widened tub edges and grab bars to make getting in and out of the bath easier
- Specially designed cooking and eating utensils that help improve grip and control tremors

SAVVY RESOURCES

You can find some assistive devices in hardware stores, discount stores, pharmacies and plumbing supply houses. Medical supply companies also stock useful items. Check your local Yellow Pages under "Medical Equipment and Supplies." Here are some Web sites that provide self-help products.

- Arthritis Store: *www.arthritisstoreusa.com*, or call 1-888-511-7367
- Assistive Devices Network: *www.assistivedevices.net*, or call 1-866-674-3549
- Beyond Hearing Aids: *www.BeyondHearingAids.com*, or call 1-800-838-1649
- Disability Products: *www.disabilityproducts.com*, or call 1-800-688-6794 access code 00
- Dynamic Living: *www.dynamic-living.com*, or call 1-888-940-0605
- Gold Violin: *www.goldviolin.com*, or call 1-877-648-8465
- Independent Living Products: *www.activeforever.com*, or call 1-800-377-8033
- Rehab Mart: *www.rehabmart.com*, or call 1-800-827-8283
- Sammons Preston: *www.sammonspreston.com*, or call 1-800-323-5547
- Solutions for Better Aging: *www.caregivers.com*, or call 1-888-405-4242
- Wellhaven, Helpful Gifts for Seniors: *www.wellhaven.com*, or call 1-610-640-3366

—Downsizing—

You never see a U-Haul following a hearse.

In our American culture, where bigger is better and more is marvelous, the idea of less is ludicrous! But the truth of the matter is that downsizing now while your health is intact is a savvy move. The process of downsizing requires a willingness to make changes and the ability to take charge of your life. It's a wise person who knows when it is the right time to let go.

 SAVVY FACT: More than 30 percent of homeowners age 65 and over have lived for 30-plus years in their home.

Where Do I Begin?

Begin by asking yourself: What would make life easier? Do I really need all this? How much space can I manage easily? Are there some possessions that could be better used and more appreciated by others? What are my financial resources?

 SAVVY TIP: Set small, achievable goals, and always keep in mind your needs versus your wants.

Downsizing Tips

If you know you'll be moving to a smaller place, consider these savvy tips.

- Make a floor plan showing each room and the placement of each piece of furniture. Try to take actual measurements of the rooms, and include locations of doors, windows, heaters, outlets, etc. Make copies of the floor plan.
- Concentrate on what you're going to take to make yourself comfortable, provide adequate storage and preserve the cozy feeling of your home.

- Assess your space-to-space needs. Where will items from built-in spaces go? If you're not taking your china cupboard, where will the china go? Will a twin bed give you more usable space than a double bed will? Problem areas are books, papers, knickknacks, linens, wardrobe and kitchen.
- Focus on sorting, separating and paring down. Be realistic: Never leave behind something you'll regret, but understand that you can't take every gift, book, blanket and mug you own (your friends and family will understand). Set a savvy goal to complete a small task every day.

Sorting

If possible, sort in place. Avoid turning your house into chaos. Have a trash bag handy; if it's trash, throw it out. If it can be donated or sold, separate it from what you're taking with you, but try to leave it in place. Pull a chair up to kitchen drawers or bookshelves. Recruit friends and family to help, especially with high shelves and hard-to-reach places. Sort things on shelves from shelf to shelf or side to side, sort drawers from drawer to drawer. Sort clothes side to side on closet rods. When you're done, things are sorted but still in place.

Letting Go

What do you do with the things you're not taking?

First, offer them to family and friends, or you might consider having a garage or yard sale. If there's lots of stuff, an estate sale may be the best way to get rid of it. Reputable estate-sale people will get the best price for your things and leave the house broom-clean for a 25–30 percent commission. Most estate-sale people will come out to see what you have for no charge.

If you consider an auction, there may be charges for transportation and insurance, and you'll still have stuff left. Small charities will come into your house, pick things up and give you a receipt for your taxes. Try to avoid lugging things to a donation center. This information was obtained in part from Busy Buddies, Inc.

- National Association of Senior Move Managers: NASMM helps with the education and advancement of the relocation options for seniors and their families. Visit them at *www.nasmm.com*.

—Senior Living Options—

Too much house and yard to take care of and the need for personal care are two of the most common reasons seniors give up their houses. If you're considering a move, it's good to know the choices available. Here is a savvy breakdown on the different retirement and assisted-living options and the basic services they provide.

Independent Living

Independent-living communities, also called retirement communities, are designed for seniors who are relatively independent both physically and socially. The major benefits seniors enjoy in this type of arrangement are maintenance-free living and socialization opportunities. Independent-living activities often include arts and crafts, exercise classes, live entertainment, movies, parties, games and outings, each adding a new dimension to the senior's experience. Other maintenance-free amenities include such things as housekeeping, transportation and meals served in a common dining area.

 SAVVY NOTE: If you go this route, you're on your own to pay for it. No insurance or federal assistance will help.

Assisted Living

This is one of the fastest-growing types of shared-living arrangements for older persons. These facilities range in size from small, home-style settings to large, full-service facilities. The idea behind assisted living is to provide specific retirement options for seniors who need more assistance than those in independent-living communities but less than those in a nursing home. The services typically include help with activities of daily living (ADL) like bathing, dressing and dining, while at the same time promoting as independent a lifestyle as each resident's limitations allow. (See Assisted-Living Facilities, page 57.)

 SAVVY NOTE: Some long-term-care insurance policies may cover some aspects of assisted-living care, but for the most part, the cost of an assisted-living facility is your responsibility.

Continuing-Care Retirement Communities (CCRC)

This type of community typically incorporates both of the above concepts while also including nursing care and possibly dementia care. The basic idea of a CCRC is that as the needs of residents change, the residents can, without leaving the community, receive appropriate care at every level. (See Continuing-Care Retirement Communities, page 59.)

 SAVVY NOTE: Most CCRCs require a onetime costly entrance fee along with a monthly rental/service fee.

Other Housing Options

- Group homes provide independent, private living in a house shared by several senior citizens who split the cost of rent, housekeeping services, utilities and meals.
- Shared housing is offered by homeowners who are willing to share their houses with others. Service provision is negotiated on a case-by-case basis.
- Adult foster care involves a family caring for a dependent person in their home. Meals, housekeeping and help with dressing, eating, bathing and other personal care are provided. Ask your local social services department if adult foster care is available in your area.

To Move or Not to Move

The main advantage of living in some type of congregate housing is security and meals. The presence of others provides continued monitoring of health care. Another big draw of such facilities, especially for those with limited mobility, are the built-in social contacts and activities. Experts agree that social contacts increase satisfaction with life and have a positive impact on physical health. Other seniors report relief at relinquishing housekeeping tasks.

Weighing the advantages of service-oriented housing against the independence offered by a single-family home is a complicated task. Timing is all-important. The most useful way to approach such decisions is to begin early by getting all the information possible on one's various options.

SENIOR LIVING RESOURCES

- Area Aging Agency: For senior housing options available in your community, call the Eldercare Locator at 1-800-677-1116 to find your local aging agency.
- HUD: Provides senior housing options for yourself, an aging parent, relative or friend. Call 1-800-569-4287 to talk to a HUD-approved housing counselor or visit *www.hud.gov*.
- American Association of Homes and Services for the Aging: They offer a consumer page containing tips on choosing facilities and services, a list of more than 5,600 senior housing facilities and community service organizations and an extensive listing of other resources. Visit *www.aahsa.org* or call 1-800-508-9442.
- Continuing Care Accreditation Commission (CCACs): The nation's only accrediting body for continuing-care retirement communities. Visit *www.ccaconline .org*.
- Senior Housing Net: Over 55,000 listings, at *www.seniorhousing.net*.
- AmericaSelect Senior Living: Call 1-504-455-7757 or see *www .marketfinder.com/amselect.html*.

- Friendly 4 Seniors: *www.friendly4seniors.com.*
- Adult Housing Leads: *www. adulthousingleads.com.*
- The Retirement Net: *www.retirenet.com.*
- The Senior Guide.com: *www.theseniorguide.com.*
- Retirement Living Information Center: *www.retirementliving.com.*
- Retirement Resorts: *www.retirementresorts.com.*
- Virtual-Retirement.com: *www.virtual-retirement.com.*

—Assisted-Living Facilities—

Need assisted-living assistance?

Assisted-living facilities are savvy options for those who can't live on their own but don't need the full-service care of a nursing home. Since there is no standard blueprint, assisted-living facilities can be different in size, appearance and the types of services they offer. For example, an assisted-living facility could be a residential home with just a few people, or a high-rise, apartment-style building with more than 200 residents. A living unit could consist of a single room or a full apartment. A facility also might be freestanding or part of a complex or cluster with a nursing home or an independent-living facility.

Assisted-Living Services

Generally, an assisted-living facility provides housing, meals, personal care and support services, social activities and some health-care services including medication management. Typical services include prepared meals in a common dining area; housekeeping, laundry and transportation services; and help with the activities of daily living, such as bathing, toileting, dressing and grooming. The extent of services and additional charges vary by facility.

Levels of Care

Assisted living is aimed at helping residents be as independent as possible while providing assistance when necessary. Since residents have varying needs, and because those needs can change over time, assisted-living facilities typically offer different levels of care at different costs. Residents of assisted-living facilities affiliated with a nursing home or rehabilitation center may have access to additional services should they require them.

Insurance

More than 80 percent of residents pay for assisted living out of their own pockets. Medicare does not cover assisted living, and while more states are beginning to cover some services under Medicaid or other government programs, public payment is not common. Although some private long-term-care insurance policies cover assisted living, only about 5 percent of Americans have such coverage.

 SAVVY NOTE: Check with your state Medicaid agency to see if any assisted-living services are covered and to find out about eligibility.

Cost

The cost for assisted living ranges anywhere from around $1,200 to as high as $5,000 a month for a private room or apartment, depending on where the facility is located, the size of the unit and the services included. Shared rooms generally cost less, ranging from about $850 to $2,000 per month. Additional services, or those not covered by the standard monthly payment, are likely to boost fees.

SAVVY NOTE: Assisted-living fees generally are not fixed: They are subject to cost-of-living increases. There also could be potential price hikes for extra services should a resident's needs change over time. This information was obtained from the Assisted Living Federation of America and AARP.

SAVVY RESOURCES

- Area Aging Agency: For senior assisted-housing options available in your community, call the Eldercare Locator at 1-800-677-1116 to find your local aging agency.
- The Assisted Living Federation of America (ALFA): Provides a list of its member facilities by each state (these are mostly for-profit facilities; the list does not include all facilities in each state). Visit *www.alfa.org* or call 1-703-691-8100.
- The American Association of Homes and Services for the Aging (AAHSA): Provides a list of member facilities by state (these are not-for-profit facilities). Call 1-202-783-2242 or visit *www.aahsa.org*.
- Check your local Yellow Pages under "Assisted-Living Facilities."

—Continuing-Care Retirement Communities—

There's no doubt that moving is a hassle and an overwhelming task for many seniors, especially if they've lived in the same house for 50 years. If you want your next move to be your last move, you need to know about Continuing-Care Retirement Communities (CCRC), also known as Life-Care Communities. This type of community is different from other housing and care options for older people because it offers a long-term contract that provides all levels of care from independent living to assisted living to skilled-nursing care, usually all in one location.

Lots of Options

CCRCs are diverse! They range from high-rises to low-rises, from simple to extravagant, from 100 residents to over 1,000. The residences may be apartments, cottages, town houses, duplexes, clusters or even single-family homes. Floor plans in a CCRC are varied, ranging from studios and one-bedrooms to two- and three-bedrooms, and larger. They are in urban, suburban and rural areas. Communities also offer many different services and programs.

CCRC Services

CCRCs provide a wide array of services tailored to each resident's needs, abilities and preferences. Typical services and amenities include

- Nursing and other health-care services
- Meals and special diets
- Housekeeping
- Scheduled transportation
- Emergency help
- Personal assistance
- Assisted living
- Recreational and educational activities

Show Me the Money

Moving into a CCRC usually requires a significant financial commitment. CCRCs usually require a onetime, costly entrance fee and monthly payments thereafter. Fees will vary greatly from one community to another, but you can expect to pay between $50,000 to $250,000 per person, depending on the type of housing and services each offers and the extent to which long-term care is covered. Other communities operate on a rental basis, in which residents make monthly payments but do not pay an entry fee. In still other communities, residents own instead of rent their units in arrangements similar to condominium or cooperative ownership. Also note that some CCRCs may provide entrance fee refunds if service or residential needs change. Be sure to check the policy at the CCRC in which you are interested.

CCRC Checklist

If you have decided that a CCRC is the best option for yourself or a family member, it's savvy advice to visit a few facilities. Here is a checklist of things to keep in mind and questions to ask as you make your decision:

- Find out what kinds of services the facility offers and which ones are included at no extra cost. Sometimes, extra services are available for additional fees.
- Inquire as to what kinds of contracts are available to you. The CCRC contract is a legal agreement between you and a continuing-care retirement community. This agreement generally secures living accommodations and services, including health-care services, over the long term. The three most common types of CCRC agreements are

   Extensive contract: Offers unlimited long-term nursing care for little or no substantial increase in your usual monthly payments.

   Modified contract: Includes a specified amount of long-term nursing care beyond which you are responsible for payment.

   Fee-for-service: You pay full daily rates for all long-term nursing care required.

- Determine what fee structure and contract option best suits your circumstances.
- Find out what the payment schedule is. Also, find out if the residents own or rent their living spaces.
- Find out if the CCRC is accredited by the Continuing Care Accreditation Commission, the only accrediting body for CCRCs.
- Before signing a contract, have your accountant or lawyer review it.

SAVVY RESOURCES

- Continuing Care Accreditation Commission (CCAC): *www.ccaconline.org*.
- American Association of Homes and Services for the Aging: Call 1-800-508-9442 or visit *www.aahsa.org*.

—Alternatives for Senior Care—

For most people, the thought of eventually ending up in a nursing home is pretty darn depressing. If you're "nursing home phobic" or not yet in need of total care, consider these other options.

Stay Home

Home and community care services can allow many seniors to remain in their homes longer with home health-care services, congregate or home-delivered meals, friendly visiting and shopper services, adult day care and the ADvantage program administered by the Department of Human Services. These programs are found in most communities.

 SAVVY NOTES: Depending on the case, Medicare, private insurance and Medicaid may pay some home-care costs that are related to medical care.

Subsidized Senior Housing

There are federal and state programs that help pay for housing for older people with low to moderate incomes. Some of these subsidized facilities offer assistance to residents who need help with certain tasks, such as shopping and laundry. Residents generally live independently in an apartment within the senior housing complex.

Assisted-Living Centers

If you only need help with a small number of tasks, such as cooking and laundry, or reminders to take medications, assisted-living facilities may be an option worth considering. (See Assisted-Living Facilities, page 57.)

Board and Care Homes

Board and care homes are group living arrangements designed to meet the needs of people who cannot live independently but do not require nursing-home services. These homes offer a wider range of services than independent-living options. Most provide help with some of the activities of daily living, including eating, walking, bathing and toileting. In some cases, private long-term-care insurance and medical-assistance programs will help pay for this type of living arrangement.

 SAVVY NOTE: Many of these homes do not get payment from Medicare or Medicaid and are not strictly monitored.

Continuing-Care Retirement Communities (CCRC)

CCRCs are housing communities that provide different levels of care based on residents' needs, from independent-living apartments to skilled-nursing care in an affiliated nursing home. (See Continuing-Care Retirement Communities, page 59.)

The Bottom Line

The options listed above may work for people who require less than skilled care, or who require skilled care for only brief periods of time. Many people with long-term-skilled-care needs require a level and amount of care that cannot be easily handled outside a nursing home.

This information was obtained in part from the Official Government Site for People with Medicare.

SAVVY RESOURCES

- Area Aging Agency: For senior housing options available in your community, call the Eldercare Locator at 1-800-677-1116 to find your local aging agency.
- HUD: Call 1-800-569-4287 to talk to a HUD-approved housing counselor or visit *www.hud.gov*.
- American Association of Homes and Services for the Aging (AAHSA): *www.aahsa.org/public/consumer.htm*.
- Senior Housing Net: Over 55,000 listings at *www.seniorhousing.net*.
- AmericaSelect Senior Living: Call 1-504-455-7757 or visit *www.marketfinder.com/amselect.html*.
- Friendly 4 Seniors: *www.friendly4seniors.com*.

- Adult Housing Leads: *www.adulthousingleads.com*.
- The Retirement Net: *www.retirenet.com*.
- The Senior Guide.com: *www.theseniorguide.com*.
- Retirement Living Information Center: *www.retirementliving.com*.

—Choosing a Nursing Home Wisely—

When it comes to choosing a quality nursing home, many people make a rushed, uninformed decision. *The Savvy Senior* advises you to know your nursing-home options and the different organizations that can help you make a sound decision and assist you if you have any problems. Here are a few tips to help you get started.

Family Involvement

Involve everyone in making this decision. This can help everyone accept this major change in your life and get themselves mentally prepared.

Location, Location, Location

Make a list of nursing homes close to people who will be visiting you frequently. Nursing-home residents with frequent visitors usually get better care!

Research Your Options

Contact the following offices about local nursing-home information and recommendations:

- **Local or state long-term-care ombudsman program:** Ombudsmen are advocates for nursing-home residents in every state and most communities. They visit nursing homes and investigate complaints. Often, ombudsmen maintain information about individual facilities. This is a great resource!

- **Nursing-home advocacy groups:** In many states, citizens have formed organizations that monitor nursing-home quality and help residents and families.
- **State or local office on aging:** These state and local agencies are sources of information about services for older persons. The long-term-care ombudsman program may be housed there.
- **Hospital discharge planners and social workers.** They maintain a list of nursing homes and often know which ones have vacancies.

Nursing-Home Cost and Medicaid

The national average cost of a nursing home today is over $50,000 a year. If you or your loved one will need financial assistance, you should probably look only at nursing homes that accept Medicaid. Most do!

Narrowing Your Choices

Once you have a short list of nursing homes, visit them. Try to visit at least three so you can make comparisons. Your visits will give you a chance to view their care first-hand; talk to the director and staff, residents and families; and taste the food. Also, be sure that the nursing homes you are considering can provide for your loved one's care and/or special needs. You might also want to consider at least one unscheduled evening and weekend visit. The element of surprise can be quite revealing!

Here are a few things to look out for when making your personal visits:

Signs of Good Care

- Cleanliness. A fresh appearance and smell.
- Dignity. Staff treating all residents—including those with dementia—with friendliness, patience and respect.
- Activity. Residents participating in a variety of activities and exercise opportunities.
- Good food. Tasty, balanced, varied meals served in pleasant surroundings.
- Helpfulness. Staff responding quickly to call bells and helping residents who need assistance with eating.

- Homelike environment. Special signs that the administration regards this as a place to continue living, not to die.

Signs of Bad Care

- Odor. Pervasive odor of urine and feces.
- Restraints. Vests, wrist restraints, wheelchair bars, locked lap trays and other devices that force people to stay in their beds and wheelchairs are dangerous and demeaning and indicate not enough or poorly trained staff.
- Lack of privacy. Residents should not be unclothed or partially clothed in rooms or hallways, and the staff should knock before entering rooms.
- Disrespect. No resident should be addressed roughly or disrespectfully.
- Unanswered calls for help.
- Resident boredom, loneliness and inactivity.
- Lack of assistance with eating.

Nursing-Home Shopping Service

Sizing up different nursing homes can be quite a confusing chore. Availability, options, cost, level of care and food quality are just a few of the issues you need to investigate as you shop and compare. To help you choose a nursing home, Medicare offers a savvy Nursing Home Compare Web site (*www.medicare.gov*) that provides visitors with information relating to Medicaid- and Medicare-certified nursing homes throughout the United States. It also includes information on payment and patient rights, and a nursing-home checklist to help you evaluate the homes you visit.

 SAVVY FACT: Two out of every five Americans will need nursing-home care at some point in their lives.

Nursing Home Compare

This Nursing Home Compare service provides an interactive tool that allows Medicare beneficiaries, their caregivers and anyone visiting the site to access comparison information about nursing homes. It contains information on every Medicare- and

Medicaid-certified nursing home in the country, including over 17,000 nationwide. Nursing Home Compare includes

- Nursing-home characteristics such as number of beds, type of ownership and whether or not the nursing home participates in Medicare, Medicaid or both.
- Resident characteristics including percent of residents with pressure sores, percent of residents with urinary incontinence and more.
- Summary information about nursing homes during their last state inspection.
- Information on the number of registered nurses, licensed practical or vocational nurses and nursing assistants in each nursing home.

Additional services offered by the Medicare nursing-home Web page include

- Nursing-Home Checklist: Rates different nursing homes visited based on quality of life, quality of care, nutrition, hydration and safety. The checklist also elaborates on how to use the information discovered through Nursing Home Compare when visiting nursing homes.
- About Nursing-Home Inspections: Explains, in more detail, the nursing-home inspection process and its goals.
- Alternatives to Nursing-Home Care: Describes the Medicare-covered programs that are available to those in need of nursing-home care but who would rather live in the comfort of their own home.
- Paying for Care: Provides basic information about Medicare, Medicaid and long-term-care insurance as they pertain to nursing-home care.
- Nursing-Home Resident Rights: Lists the rights, by law, of all nursing-home patients.

 SAVVY FACT: After age 65, a woman's chance of eventually needing nursing-home care is 52 percent, versus 35 percent for a man. Why the disparity? Because women live longer than men.

This information was obtained in part from Medicare and AARP.

SAVVY RESOURCES

- Area Aging Agency: Ask about recommended long-term-care facilities in your community and where you can get more information on Medicaid. Call the Eldercare Locator at 1-800-677-1116 to find your local aging agency.

- Center for Medicaid and Medicare Services (CMS): A 37-page booklet with information on how to choose a nursing home is available free. Call 1-800-Medicare (1-800-633-4227) or view it on the Web at *www.cms.gov*.

- The National Citizens' Coalition for Nursing Home Reform: They can tell you how to contact the long-term-care ombudsman, any citizen advocacy groups and the nursing-home survey and certification agency in your state. The coalition also publishes a book, *Nursing Homes: Getting Good Care There*, and fact sheets and booklets for friends and families of nursing-home residents. Call 1-202-332-2275 or visit *www.nccnhr.org*.

- American Association of Homes and Services for the Aging: They provide information and the publication "Guide to Finding the Right Nursing Home." Log on to *www.aahsa.org/public/sh.htm*.

- American Health Care Association/National Center for Assisted Living: Provides consumer information to assist individuals in making decisions regarding nursing homes and assisted-living facilities. Visit *www.longtermcareliving .com/planning_ahead/index.htm*.

— Ombudsmen —

Nursing homes across America, for the most part, provide quality care for their residents. But as they say, bad things do happen to good people! If you know of or suspect any nursing-home or senior-care-facility neglect or abuse, contact your local long-term-care ombudsman program so they can nip it in the bud.

LTC Ombudsmen

Long-term-care ombudsmen are super-savvy advocates for residents of nursing homes, board and care homes, assisted-living facilities and similar adult-care facilities. Ombudsmen work to resolve problems of individual residents and to bring about changes to improve care. While most residents receive good care in long-term-care facilities, far too many are neglected, and other unfortunate incidents of psychological, physical and other kinds of abuse do occur. Thus, thousands of trained volunteer ombudsmen regularly visit long-term-care facilities, monitor conditions and care and provide a voice for those unable to speak for themselves.

Begun in 1972 as a demonstration program, the Ombudsman Program today is established in all states under the Older Americans Act, which is administered by the Administration on Aging (AoA). The long-term-care Ombudsmen Program has almost 1,000 paid ombudsmen and 8,000 certified volunteer ombudsmen, working in 591 localities nationwide.

Ombudsmen have investigated about 232,000 complaints made by 137,000 individuals and provided information on long-term care to another 245,000 people. The most frequent complaints have been those involving lack of resident care due to inadequate staffing.

Residents' Rights

Ombudsmen help residents and their families and friends understand and exercise rights that are guaranteed by law. Residents have the right to

- Be treated with respect and dignity.
- Be free from chemical and physical restraints.
- Manage their own finances.
- Voice grievances without fear of retaliation.
- Associate and communicate privately with any person of their choice.
- Send and receive personal mail.
- Have personal and medical records kept confidential.
- Apply for state and federal assistance without discrimination.

- Be fully informed, prior to admission, of their rights, services available and all charges.
- Be given advance notice of transfer or discharge.

Ombudsman Responsibilities

Ombudsmen are required to

- Identify, investigate and resolve complaints made by or on behalf of residents.
- Provide information to residents about long-term-care services.
- Represent the interests of residents before governmental agencies and seek administrative, legal and other remedies to protect residents.
- Analyze, comment on and recommend changes in laws and regulations pertaining to the health, safety, welfare and rights of residents.
- Educate and inform consumers and the general public regarding issues and concerns related to long-term care and facilitate public comment on laws, regulations, policies and actions.
- Promote the development of citizen organizations to participate in the program.
- Provide technical support for the development of resident and family councils to protect the well-being and rights of residents.
- Advocate for changes to improve residents' quality of life and care.

Contact Information

For more information on your local Ombudsman Program, or to become an ombudsman volunteer, contact your state or local long-term-care ombudsman. To get the phone number in your area, call your Eldercare Locator at 1-800-677-1116. You can also contact the National Long Term Care Ombudsman Resource Center. They provide on-call technical assistance and many resources to assist residents and their families. For information, call 1-202-332-2275 or log on to *www.nccnhr.org* and click on "Ombudsmen Resources."

—Intergenerational Living—

Intergenerational living refers to when an aging parent lives with their adult child and his or her family. Needless to say, this brings up some very interesting issues.

The key to intergenerational living is intergenerational communication. Be sure everyone involved knows the possible consequences of living in an extended-family situation. Before you make the move, carefully weigh the pros and cons of living together. Every family's situation is unique.

Following is a listing of some of the benefits and drawbacks of the intergenerational experience.

Benefits

- If considerable care is needed, you will save the expense of a long-term-care facility or at least some in-home services.
- You know that your parent is getting the best possible care because you are either providing it yourself or directly overseeing it.
- You will be able to make major decisions, which can give you a sense of empowerment.
- You will have more time to spend with your family member.
- Your children will have an opportunity to spend more time with their grandparent, have an important lesson in compassion and responsibility, learn about their roots and develop a sense of family continuity.
- If your parent is up to it, he or she may help with household tasks or with the children.

Drawbacks

- You may have less time for yourself and/or other family members, and if you work you may find conflicts between your job and caregiving responsibilities.
- You will lose at least some of your privacy.

- Other family members may resent the new arrangement.
- There may be less space for everyone in the family.
- You may find that hands-on caregiving is too physically and/or emotionally demanding.
- Depending on your lifelong relationship with your family member, you may find that, in time, you resent the changes that may take place.

Things to Ponder

- Is your home large enough so that everyone can have privacy when they want it?
- Is there a separate bedroom and bath for your family member, or can you create an accessory apartment?
- Are these rooms on the first floor? If not, can your relative climb stairs safely?
- Can you add to or remodel your home to provide a first-floor bedroom and bath?
- Do you need to add safety features such as ramps and better lighting?
- Does the bathroom have a shower; is it large enough to accommodate a wheelchair, if needed? Can you install safety features, such as grab bars, to prevent falls?
- Are door openings wide enough for a wheelchair?

 SAVVY NOTE: If you do decide to give it a try, you might want to try it on a trial basis, if possible.

SAVVY RESOURCES

- Area Aging Agency: Ask about the caregiving options and community services available to older adults in your community. Call the Eldercare Locator at 1-800-677-1116 to find your local aging agency.
- Family Caregiver Alliance: a support and resource organization for caregivers, at *www.caregiver.org*.

- National Alliance for Caregiving: A National Resource on Caregiving. Visit *www.caregiving.org*.
- CareGuide: Offers a full range of services, articles and resources for children of aging parents: *www.careguide.net*.
- Children of Aging Parents: Provides information and referral services for support groups, and educational outreach services. Call 1-800-227-7294 or visit *www.caps4caregivers.org*.
- AARP Caregivers Circle Discussion Board: Share practical tips and express your ideas, ask questions, tell a story, share a frustration at *www.aarp.org*.
- Administration on Aging: A resource guide for the growing number of people who are caring for older family members. See *www.aoa.dhhs.gov/caregivers*.

—Long-Distance Caregiving—

In today's mobile American society, long-distance caregiving is becoming more and more common. If you have the responsibility of overseeing your parent's or loved one's care from a distance, here are some savvy suggestions that might help out.

What to Do

Determine with your loved one, and perhaps other family members, what assistance they need, such as

- Opportunities to socialize.
- Help with chores or housekeeping.
- Personal-care help, such as bathing or dressing.
- Fixing meals.
- Legal assistance with money or health-care matters.
- Help taking care of money matters and paying bills.

- Medications and medical checkups.
- Transportation.
- Changes to the home.

Where to Turn

Gather information on community services that can meet your needs. You can get a lot of information over the phone and the Internet. Start with the resources listed below for organizations that can help.

 SAVVY TIP: Consider finding a geriatric-care manager to help assess and manage your parents' care. A care manager can be located by the Eldercare Locator or through the National Association of Professional Geriatric Care Managers. (See Geriatric-Care Manager, page 75.)

Whom to Call

Identify friends, neighbors, clergy and others in regular contact with your loved one. Introduce yourself to close friends or neighbors and keep a list of their phone numbers and addresses. If for some reason you can't reach your loved one or are concerned, calling their friends and neighbors can help to ease your mind. They also may be able to help with shopping, transportation or visits.

What to Know (Before a Crisis Occurs)

- **Medical:** Medical conditions, medications, doctors' names and phone numbers.
- **Financial:** A list of what your parents own and their debts, with dollar values, yearly income and expenses, a statement of net worth, information on bank accounts or other financial holdings and credit card information.
- **Legal:** Other relevant documents they have or want to create (will, advance directives), where they keep important documents (birth certificates, insurance policies, Social Security numbers, drivers' licenses).

Home Visits

Talk with your parent so that you can decide together what needs to be done and who can help. Be observant while you are visiting. Do you notice anything unusual? Are they eating nutritious meals regularly? Are finances in good order? Are there any obvious health or safety problems?

 SAVVY NOTE: Be sensitive to your loved one's situation throughout this process. They may be concerned about having strangers in their home or have trouble facing change. Always remember to treat them the same way you would want to be treated.

RESOURCES

- Area Aging Agency: Ask about caregiving options available in your community. Call the Eldercare Locator at 1-800-677-1116 to find your local aging agency.
- American Association of Homes and Services for the Aging (AAHS): Offers a directory and tips on choosing facilities and services. Visit *www.aahsa.org/public/consumer.htm.*

—Geriatric-Care Manager—

Living far from an elderly loved one in need can be frustrating and paralyzing. If you are a long-distance caregiver, you need to know about geriatric-care managers, a savvy service for aging seniors.

What Is a Geriatric-Care Manager?

A geriatric-care manager (GCM) is a professional who specializes in assisting older people and their families in meeting their long-term-care arrangements. GCMs usually have training in gerontology, social work, nursing or counseling. Depending on what you need, a GCM can help

- Conduct care-planning assessments to identify problems, eligibility for assistance and need for services.
- Screen, arrange and monitor in-home help or other services.
- Review financial, legal and medical issues and offer referrals to geriatric specialists to avoid future problems and conserve assets.
- Provide crisis intervention.
- Act as a liaison to families at a distance, making sure things are going well and alerting families to problems.
- Assist with moving an older person to or from a retirement complex, care home or nursing home.
- Provide consumer education and advocacy.
- Offer counseling and support.

Some GCMs also provide family or individual therapy, money management and conservatorship or guardianship assistance. GCMs also have extensive knowledge about the costs, quality and availability of services in the community.

 SAVVY NOTE: Some GCMs specialize in assessments and care consultation but don't follow people on an ongoing basis.

Choosing a GCM

Choose carefully! The field of geriatric-care management is relatively unregulated and many people without specialized training can identify themselves as care managers, care coordinators or care advisers. So it is wise to screen the candidates thoroughly to ensure that you're working with a qualified professional. Here are some good questions to ask a prospective care manager:

- What are your professional credentials?
- Are you licensed in your profession?
- Are you a member of the National Association of Professional Geriatric Care Managers?
- How long have you been providing care-management services?

- What is your average response time to calls from clients and their families?
- What is your method of communication: pager, cell phone, answering service or voice mail? How will you communicate information to me?
- Does your company also provide home-care services?
- Are you available for emergencies, and how are after-hour emergencies handled?
- What are the backup systems for covering vacations and days off?
- Will we be working with one or several GCMs?
- What are your fees? (These should be provided in writing to the responsible party prior to services starting.)
- What are your references?

GCM Cost

Cost will vary depending on the scope of services you choose and where you live, but you can expect to spend between $200 and $350 for a client assessment and a $40- to $150-per-hour rate.

How to Find a GCM

There are several sources you can use to locate a good geriatric-care manager, including

- Area Aging Agency: Call the Eldercare Locator at 1-800-677-1116 to locate the geriatric-care managers in your area.
- National Association of Professional Geriatric Care Managers: Visit their Web site at *www.caremanager.org*.
- Hospitals, senior centers, geriatric assessment centers and charitable organizations, such as the Alzheimer's Association, are all good possible sources.

—Alzheimer's Caregivers—

Despite the widespread belief that most people with Alzheimer's disease (AD) reside in nursing homes, family members are actually the primary caregivers, most often wives and husbands.

 SAVVY FACT: According to the Alzheimer's Association, of the 4 million Americans who suffer from AD, about 70 percent live at home.

The Right Time

There is no rule regarding the "right time" to place a person with AD in a more protective environment or nursing home. This decision requires careful consideration by the caregiver of the person's needs and the caregiver's ability to manage the person's care safely. *The Savvy Senior* recommends consulting with your doctor or other savvy professionals to help you make a wise decision.

Home-Modification Tips

Caregivers of people with AD often have to look at their homes through new eyes to identify and correct safety risks. Here are a few tips that can help prevent stressful and dangerous situations.

- Install secure locks on all outside doors and windows, especially if the person is prone to wandering. Remove the locks on bathroom doors to prevent the person from accidentally locking him- or herself in.
- Use childproof latches on kitchen cabinets and any place where cleaning supplies or other chemicals are kept.
- Label medications and keep them locked up. Also make sure knives, lighters, matches and guns are secured and out of reach.
- Keep the house free from clutter. Remove scatter rugs and anything else that might contribute to a fall. Make sure lighting is good both inside and out.

- Consider installing an automatic shutoff switch on the stove to prevent burns or fire.
- Remove plug-in appliances from the kitchen and bathroom to avoid the risk of electric shock, and set water heater temperature no higher than 120° F to prevent burns.
- Install handrails to prevent falls.
- If your loved one can no longer drive, control access to car keys and keep the car out of sight.
- Avoid rearranging furniture.

Support

State and county agencies on aging are a good source of information about support services for caregivers. They can provide information on nursing homes, adult day-care centers, assisted-living facilities, attendant care and caseworker services. They can also provide information on respite care, home health care, homemakers, chore services and Meals on Wheels.

This information was obtained from the Alzheimer's Association, the National Institute on Aging Information Center and the Alzheimer's Disease Education and Referral (ADEAR) Center.

SAVVY RESOURCES

- Alzheimer's Association: This nonprofit association supports families and care-givers of patients with AD. Almost 300 chapters nationwide provide referrals to local resources and services, and sponsor support groups and educational programs. Online and print versions of publications also are available. Call 1-800-272-3900 or see their Web site at *www.alz.org*.
- Alzheimer's Disease Education and Referral (ADEAR) Center: Offers information and publications on diagnosis, treatment, patient care, caregiver needs, long-term care, education and training, and research related to AD. Call 1-800-438-4380 or see their Web site at *www.alzheimers.org*.

- Area Aging Agency: Provides older persons and their caregivers with specific information about services in the community. Call the Eldercare Locator at 1-800-677-1116.
- Family Caregiver Alliance: a support and resource organization for caregivers at *www.caregiver.org*.
- CareGuide: Offers a full range of services, articles and resources for children of aging parents: *www.careguide.net*.

HEALTH

HEALTH IS SUCH A HUGE ISSUE FOR MOST SENIORS THAT IT BRINGS TO mind the old saying, "Getting old is definitely not for sissies." Understanding and managing the many changes in health that occur as we age is what this section is all about. Can you recognize the signs of stroke, or the subtle symptoms of a heart attack? What about arthritis or Alzheimer's? Has your mother had a recent bone density scan for osteoporosis? Maybe your spouse is acting peculiar and you suspect dementia or Alzheimer's disease, or he or she is simply depressed to find out that retirement can be overrated.

Part of aging means not only managing health issues but also maintaining health and fitness. It may surprise you that lifting weights is recommended for all ages, including seniors. So is eating balanced meals and ensuring quality rest, getting flu shots, regular eye care, dental care and much more.

— Senior Eye Care —

Did you know that by age 65, one in three Americans has some form of vision-impairing eye disease? Most, however, do not know it, because often there are no warning symptoms, or because they assume that poor sight is a natural part of growing older. By detecting and treating eye disease early through annual dilated-eye exams, seniors can preserve their sight.

EyeCare America

Have you heard about EyeCare America? It's a Senior EyeCare Program (SEP) that offers medical eye care to all eligible seniors and promotes annual dilated-eye exams. SEP also raises awareness about age-related eye disease, including cataracts; and provides free eye-care educational materials and facilitates access to eye care.

People eligible for a referral through the program receive a comprehensive medical eye exam and up to one year of treatment, at no out-of-pocket expense, for any condition diagnosed during the initial exam. Volunteer ophthalmologists will accept Medicare or other insurance as full payment, with no additional payment from you.

 SAVVY NOTE: Eyeglasses, prescriptions, hospital services and fees of other medical professionals are not covered.

The Seniors EyeCare Program is designed for people who

- Are U.S. citizens or legal residents,
- Are age 65 and older,
- Have not seen an ophthalmologist in three or more years, and
- Do not have eye-care insurance through an HMO or the VA.

 SAVVY NOTE: Each year, 12,000–24,000 people become blind because of diabetic eye disease. Screening and care can prevent up to 90 percent of diabetes-related blindness; however, only 60 percent of people with diabetes receive annual dilated-eye exams.

Services

The greatest benefit of the SEP is that it encourages financially disadvantaged seniors to take care of vision problems before they get worse. Cataracts need to be monitored and eventually removed; glaucoma and ocular hypertension must be treated regularly. Left untreated, these diseases often lead to blindness.

 SAVVY TIP: EyeCare America also offers a Glaucoma EyeCare Program (GEP), a Diabetes EyeCare Program (DEP) and a Children's EyeCare Program (CEP).

Contact Information

To determine if you, a family member or friend qualify for a SEP referral, or to get the name of an ophthalmologist participating in the SEP in your area, call 1-800-222-EYES (1-800-222-3937), 24 hours a day, 365 days a year, or visit *www.eyecareamerica.org.*

EYE CARE RESOURCES

- VISION USA: Coordinated by the American Optometric Association (AOA), VISION USA provides free eye care to uninsured, low-income workers and their families. Call 1-800-766-4466 or visit *www.aoa.org.*
- Lions Clubs International provides financial assistance to individuals for eye care through local clubs. There are Lions Clubs in most localities, though services vary from club to club. Check your telephone book for the number of your local club, or call 1-800-74 SIGHT (1-800-747-4448) or visit *www.lionsclubs .org.*
- Mission Cataract USA: Coordinated by the Volunteer Eye Surgeons' Association, this program provides free cataract surgery to people of all ages who have no other means to pay. Surgeries are scheduled annually, usually in May. Call 1-800-343-7265.
- LensCrafters Gift of Sight: LensCrafters doctors and associates collect and recycle old glasses, offer vision screening at health fairs and provide new glasses to preselected needy people in LensCrafters stores and their two mobile

"Vision Vans." To learn more, contact the Gift of Sight store captain at the LensCrafters store nearest you. For an online store locator, visit *www .lenscrafters.com/store_locator.html* or call 1-800-541-LENS (1-800-541-5367).

- Knights Templar Eye Foundation: A partner with Eye Care America, the Knights Templar Eye Foundation is a charitable foundation that provides financial assistance to those who need surgical treatment to prevent vision loss. For more information and eligibility requirements, call 1-773-205-3838 or visit *www.knightstemplar.org*.

- New Eyes for the Needy provides vouchers for the purchase of new prescription eyeglasses. Write to them at 549 Millburn Avenue, P.O. Box 332, Short Hills, NJ 07078-0332, or call 1-973-376-4903.

—Stroke Signs—

Every second counts where a stroke is concerned. Knowing the warning signs and getting to the hospital quickly can make a difference in how much and how quickly a stroke patient recovers.

It's a fact that stroke patients who receive treatment within three hours of their initial symptoms are at least 30 percent more likely to recover with little or no disability.

Few other medical conditions come on so suddenly or are so noticeable to a bystander than is a major stroke. The sooner a stroke is diagnosed and the patient begins receiving medication, the better the chances for a complete recovery. Remember, every second counts!

 SAVVY NOTE: The medication used in many stroke patients is called tissue plasminogen activator (TPA), which dissolves the clots that cause most strokes.

Facts about Stroke

Stroke is the third leading cause of death in the United States and the leading cause of serious, long-term disability. Approximately 600,000 new strokes are reported in the United States annually, and about 160,000 Americans die each year from stroke.

What Is a Stroke?

A stroke occurs when the blood supply to a part of the brain is suddenly interrupted or when a blood vessel in the brain bursts, spilling blood into the spaces surrounding the brain cells. Without oxygen and important nutrients, the affected brain cells are either damaged or die within a few minutes. The effects of a stroke may be very slight or severe, temporary or permanent. It depends on which brain cells have been damaged, how widespread the damage is, how well the body repairs the blood supply system to the brain, or how quickly other areas of brain tissue take over the work of the damaged cells.

Stroke Warning Signs

- Weakness or numbness of face, arm or leg on one side
- Trouble talking or understanding others when they talk
- Changes in eyesight such as dimness, double vision or loss of vision
- Dizziness, unsteadiness or sudden falls
- Sudden, severe headache

 SAVVY TIP: If you recognize any of these symptoms, **call 911**.

Your Risk for Stroke Is Higher If

- You are over the age of 65,
- You are a male,
- People in your family have had strokes,
- You are African American, or
- You have had a previous stroke.

Treatable Risk Factors for Stroke

- High blood pressure
- Irregular heartbeat
- Heart failure
- Being overweight
- Smoking
- High cholesterol
- Heavy alcohol use

Mini-Stroke Warning

According to the American Stroke Association, more than 500,000 people in the United States have mini-strokes each year. A mini-stroke, also known as a transient ischemic attack (TIA), occurs when the blood supply to part of the brain is briefly interrupted. TIA symptoms, which usually occur suddenly, are similar to those of stroke but don't last as long. Symptoms may be subtle but can include paralysis and numbness, vision and speech problems, dizziness and headaches. But the symptoms go away in less than a day and leave no lasting damage, which is why they are easily ignored.

 SAVVY NOTE: People who have mini-strokes are 10 times more likely to have a major stroke in the future, and for many it will come within a month to a year after the mini-stroke.

SAVVY RESOURCES

- National Institute of Neurological Disorders and Strokes (NINDS): Call 1-800-352-9424 or visit *www.ninds.nih.gov*.
- American Stroke Association: Call 1-888-4-STROKE (1-888-478-7653) or visit *www.strokeassociation.org*.
- National Stroke Association: Call 1-800-STROKES (1-800-787-6537) or visit *www.stroke.org*.

—Subtle Heart-Attack Symptoms—

Heart disease does not discriminate! While most Americans may still associate a *heart attack* with the image of an overweight, overstressed, red-faced, middle-aged man, in fact, more women than men die of heart disease each year. Here are some savvy things you should know about this number one killer of both men and women.

 SAVVY FACT: One in two women will eventually die of heart disease or stroke, compared with one in 30 who will eventually die of breast cancer.

Am I Having a Heart Attack?

It's not uncommon for people to have a heart attack and not even know it. Signs of a heart attack can vary from person to person; however, women and diabetics are the ones who are more likely to experience subtle symptoms that make it difficult to recognize an attack is taking place.

Symptoms

Classic heart-attack symptoms include

- Uncomfortable pressure, fullness, squeezing or pain in the center of the chest that lasts more than a few minutes or that goes away and comes back;
- Pain or discomfort in one or both arms, the back, neck, jaw or stomach; and
- Chest discomfort with lightheadedness, fainting, sweating, nausea or shortness of breath.

Some women have fewer chest pain symptoms than men but experience other symptoms, such as

- Atypical chest, back, stomach or abdominal pain;
- Nausea or dizziness;
- Unexplained anxiety and nervousness, weakness or overwhelming tiredness;

- Cold, sweaty skin and pallor; or
- Swelling of the ankles and/or lower legs.

 SAVVY NOTE: Many women mistakenly think only crushing chest pain is a symptom of a heart attack and, therefore, delay seeking medical care. Others have found that their doctor made a mistake and failed to recognize their heart-attack symptoms, telling them to go home and rest or that it is probably just indigestion or heartburn. That's why it is so important for you to insist that the doctor administer an EKG test or an enzyme blood test to see if you are having a heart attack. Don't be shy—it's your heart, and your life!

What Is a Heart Attack?

A heart attack occurs when the blood supply to part of the heart muscle is severely reduced or stopped due to blockage of one or more of the coronary arteries that supply blood to the heart muscle. The blockage is usually from the buildup of plaque deposits along the artery wall. The plaque tears or ruptures, triggering the formation of a blood clot that blocks the artery and leads to an attack.

SAVVY FACT: Most heart attacks take place in the morning between 4 and 10 A.M.

Doctors still don't know why attacks manifest differently in women, but they do know that the risk accelerates after menopause. As a woman gets older, her body produces lesser amounts of estrogen, which helps maintain higher levels of "good" cholesterol and reduces blood pressure. In the case of diabetics, "silent" attacks usually occur because the diabetes affects victims' nerves, diminishing their ability to feel the symptoms. Diabetic women need to be extra careful.

Time Is Muscle

When it comes to heart attacks, the longer you wait, the more damage is done to your heart muscle. If you get to an emergency room soon enough, you can literally stop the attack. Don't worry about the possibility of being wrong. Remember that fast action saves lives.

SAVVY RESOURCES

- American Heart Association: Call 1-800-242-8721 or visit *www.americanheart.org.*
- National Coalition for Women with Heart Disease: *www.womenheart.org.*
- National Heart, Lung and Blood Institute: Call 1-301-496-4236 or visit *www.nhlbi.nih.gov.*
- National Heart Savers Association: *www.heartsavers.org.*
- The Heart Cardiology Online: *www.theheart.org.*

—CRP Test—
PREVENTIVE MEASURES FOR HEART HEALTH

Have you had your cholesterol checked lately? How about your C-reactive protein? If not, it's savvy advice to have both checked. Here's why: New studies show that painless inflammation deep within the body is the single most powerful trigger of heart attacks, worse even than high cholesterol.

Savvy Study

Published in the *New England Journal of Medicine,* a study followed almost 28,000 women for eight years. Fully 77 percent of those who had heart attacks or strokes had cholesterol in the normal range and 45 percent were in the ideal range.

The study also included a separate blood test that measures something called C-reactive protein, or CRP, a measure of inflammation deep within the body. The study found that the CRP test actually did a better job of predicting heart-disease risk than cholesterol. Those with high levels of inflammation are twice as likely as those with high cholesterol to die from heart attacks and strokes.

Hypothesis

With this latest study, many believe the evidence is overwhelming that inflammation is a central factor in cardiovascular disease. Doctors believe inflammation has many possible sources. Often, the fatty buildup that lines the blood vessels becomes inflamed as white blood cells invade in a misguided defense attempt. Fat cells are also known to turn out these inflammatory proteins. Other possible triggers include high blood pressure, smoking and lingering low-level infections, such as chronic gum disease.

Inflammation is thought to weaken the fatty buildup, or plaque deposits, making them more likely to rupture. A piece of plaque can then lead to a clot that can choke off the blood flow and cause a heart attack.

CRP Test Results

Experts are still divided over which patients to test and how to treat them if their CRP readings are high. Talk to your doctor or pharmacist about the CRP blood test.

 SAVVY NOTE: The CRP test can be tricky; it can jump as much as tenfold when a person is fighting a cold or flu, and it shouldn't be used in place of a cholesterol test.

Tips to Lower Inflammation Levels

- Eat sensibly and exercise. Inactivity and obesity increase inflammatory proteins that can trigger heart attacks. People can substantially lower their levels of these proteins simply by improving their living habits.
- Consume moderate amounts of alcohol and fish oil.
- Do not smoke.
- Keep your blood pressure under control.
- Cholesterol-lowering drugs called statins can reduce the inflammation, and so does a daily dose of aspirin (check with your doctor first).

- U.S. Department of Health and Human Services—National Institutes of Health: *www.nih.gov*
- The Centers for Disease Control and Prevention (CDC): *www.cdc.gov*

—Alzheimer's and Other Forms of Dementia—

According to the Alzheimer's Disease Education and Referral (ADEAR) Center, a lot of people experience memory lapses. However, most people remain both alert and able as they age, although it may take them longer to remember things. People who have serious changes in their memory, personality and behavior may suffer from a form of dementia. Alzheimer's disease is just one of many types of dementia.

Dementia Symptoms Include

- Asking the same questions repeatedly,
- Becoming lost in familiar places,
- Being unable to follow directions,
- Getting disoriented about time, people and places, and
- Neglecting personal safety, hygiene and nutrition.

 SAVVY NOTE: People with dementia lose their abilities at different rates.

If this is you or someone you know, **call your doctor!**

Dementia is caused by many conditions, including some that can be treated and reversed, and others that cannot. Some of the treatable conditions can be caused by a high fever, dehydration, vitamin deficiency, poor nutrition, bad reactions to medicines, problems with the thyroid gland or a minor head injury. Also, sometimes older people have emotional problems that can be mistaken for dementia. Feeling sad, lonely, worried or bored may be more common for older people facing retirement or coping with the death of a spouse, relative or friend. Adapting to these changes leaves some people feeling confused or forgetful.

Forms of Dementia

The two most common forms of dementia are Alzheimer's disease and multi-infarct dementia (sometimes called vascular dementia). These types of dementia cannot be cured.

- Alzheimer's Disease: With this disease, nerve-cell changes in certain parts of the brain result in the death of a large number of cells. Symptoms of Alzheimer's disease begin slowly and become steadily worse. As the disease progresses, symptoms range from mild forgetfulness to serious impairments in thinking, judgment and the ability to perform daily activities. Eventually, patients may need total care.
- Multi-Infarct Dementia: A series of small strokes or changes in the brain's blood supply may result in the death of brain tissue. Symptoms that begin suddenly may be a sign of this kind of dementia. People with multi-infarct dementia are likely to show signs of improvement or remain stable for long periods of time, then quickly develop new symptoms if more strokes occur. In many people with multi-infarct dementia, high blood pressure is to blame.

 SAVVY NOTE: Alzheimer's disease and multi-infarct dementia can exist together, making it hard for a doctor to diagnose either one specifically.

Treatment

Even if a doctor diagnoses an irreversible form of dementia, much can still be done to treat the patient and help the family cope. For some people in the early and middle stages of Alzheimer's disease, four medications—Aricept, Exelon, Reminyl and Cognexare—are currently available. These drugs can work to possibly delay the worsening of some of the disease's symptoms. The Food and Drug Administration has also recently approved a new drug specifically for people in the late stages of Alzheimer's disease called memantine, which will be sold in the United States under the brand name Namenda.

 SAVVY TIP: Doctors believe it is very important for people with multi-infarct dementia to try to prevent further strokes by controlling high blood pressure.

Advice for Now

Scientists are working to develop new drugs that one day may slow, reverse or prevent the damage caused by Alzheimer's disease and multi-infarct dementia. In the meantime, people who have no dementia symptoms can try to keep their memory sharp by developing interests or hobbies and staying involved in activities that stimulate both the mind and the body. Here are a few activities to consider.

Dancing

Believe it or not, dancing is one of many activities that may help delay the onset of Alzheimer's because it requires both physical and mental abilities. What's more, it's good for your heart, and soul mate, too. Other mentally stimulating activities include

- Chess
- Playing a musical instrument
- Puzzles
- Reading

Done regularly, these activities exercise and even strengthen the brain.

 SAVVY TIP: Don't forget your greens and grains. Along with all those other habits we tried to instill in our children, such as reading and playing the piano, this advice may have an unexpected benefit as well. Turns out there may be a link between leafy vegetables and other foods rich in vitamin E and battling Alzheimer's. So eat healthy, tickle the ivories and take a good mystery to bed with you when you get home.

- Area Aging Agency: Ask for information about local community Alzheimer's resources. Call the Eldercare Locator at 1-800-677-1116 to find your local aging agency.
- The Alzheimer's Disease Education and Referral (ADEAR) Center: Call 1-800-438-4380 or visit *www.alzheimers.org/adear*.
- The Alzheimer's Association: Call 1-800-272-3900 or visit *www.alz.org* for information and referrals to support groups.

—Arthritis and Exercise—

If you suffer from arthritis pain, you might consider taking a walk!

Savvy studies have shown that exercise helps people with arthritis by reducing joint pain and stiffness, and by increasing flexibility, muscle strength, cardiac fitness and endurance. Along with exercise, other treatment plans include rest and relaxation, proper diet, medication and instruction about the proper way to move joints and how to conserve your body's energy.

Suitable Exercises

- Range-of-motion exercises help maintain normal joint movement and relieve stiffness. This type of exercise also helps maintain or increase flexibility.
- Strengthening exercises help keep or increase muscle strength. Strong muscles help support and protect joints affected by arthritis.
- Aerobic or endurance exercises improve cardiovascular fitness, help control weight and improve overall function. Weight control can be important because the extra weight puts extra pressure on many joints. Some studies show that aerobic exercise can reduce inflammation in some joints.

Tips on Arthritis and Exercise

- Discuss exercise plans with your doctor.
- Start with supervision from a physical therapist or qualified athletic trainer.
- Apply heat to sore joints before exercising (optional).
- Stretch and warm up with range-of-motion exercises.
- Start strengthening exercises slowly with small weights (a one- or two-pound weight can make a big difference).
- Progress slowly.
- Use cold packs after exercising (optional).
- Add aerobic exercise.
- Consider appropriate recreational exercise (after doing range-of-motion, strengthening and aerobic exercises). Fewer injuries to joints affected by arthritis occur during recreational exercise if it is preceded by range-of-motion, strengthening and aerobic exercise that gets your body in the best condition possible.
- Ease off if joints become painful, inflamed or red, and work with your doctor to find the cause and treat it.
- Choose the exercise program you enjoy most and make it a habit.

☞ **SAVVY NOTE:** Always consult with your doctor before starting an exercise program. This information was obtained from the U.S. Department of Health and Human Services—National Institutes of Health.

SAVVY RESOURCES

- Arthritis Foundation: Publishes a free pamphlet on exercise and arthritis and a monthly magazine for members. Call 1-800-283-7800 or visit *www.arthritis.org*.
- American Academy of Orthopedic Surgeons: The academy publishes free brochures on arthritis subjects. Call 1-800-824-2663 or visit *www.aaos.org*.
- People with Arthritis Can Exercise (PACE): Sells exercise videotapes at two levels, basic and advanced. Call 1-800-722-3236.

- National Institute of Arthritis and Musculoskeletal and Skin Diseases Information Clearinghouse (NIAMS): Call toll-free 1-877-226-4268 or visit *www.nih/gov/niams.*

—Remember Your Flu Shot—

Did you know that each winter, the flu is responsible for killing, on average, 20,000 Americans, most of them over age 65? Don't let this include you!

 SAVVY NOTE: Currently only 65 percent of seniors receive their annual flu shot.

Flu Season

Just like the holidays, flu season comes around every year. In the United States, flu season typically runs from October through April. The U.S. Centers for Disease Control and Prevention (CDC) recommends that anyone who wants to lower his or her chances of getting the flu should get a flu shot (the shot can be administered to children as young as 6 months).

Although the flu is a common illness, it can be dangerous. This is especially true for people age 65 and older or those with certain illnesses or compromised immune systems. For those at greater risk of getting the flu and related complications, the CDC recommends getting a flu shot between September and mid-November.

 SAVVY NOTE: Even January is not too late to be vaccinated against the flu. Because different types of flu viruses keep developing, it's important to get a flu shot every year.

Flu Shots

A flu shot can prevent between 70 and 90 percent of flu illnesses, according to the CDC. However, it will not prevent illnesses with flu-like symptoms caused by a non-flu virus. The flu vaccine is safe for most people. According to the CDC, the only people who should avoid the shot are those who've had allergic reactions to eggs, bad reactions to previous flu shots or a history of Guillain-Barré Syndrome. Talk to your doctor if you have concerns about the shot.

 SAVVY NOTE: Flu shots must be given every year because the influenza virus changes from year to year and because antibody protection from the vaccine wanes over time.

Side Effects

The vaccine's most common side effect is soreness at the vaccination site for up to two days. Some people may experience post-shot fever, sore muscles and other symptoms resembling the flu that can last for one to two days. But the flu vaccine cannot actually cause flu, because it contains only inactivated viruses.

Where Do I Go?

You can get a flu shot at your doctor's office or a local clinic. Many communities also offer flu shots at supermarkets and drugstores. If you are not sure where to get a flu shot in your area, call your county health department or call the CDC hotline at 1-800-232-2522 for help.

Who Should Not Get a Flu Shot

The following groups should not get a flu shot before talking with their doctor:

- People who have a severe allergy to hens' eggs.
- People who have had a severe reaction to a flu shot in the past.
- People who previously developed Guillain-Barré Syndrome (GBS) in the six weeks after getting a flu shot.

Medicare Coverage

Since 1993, flu shots for the elderly have been free for those enrolled in Medicare Part B, given by physicians who accept Medicare payment as full payment. Medicare also covers vaccinations against pneumonia. For more information about receiving a flu shot covered by Medicare, call 1-800-638-6833 or visit Medicare's Web site at *www.medicare.gov.* This information was obtained in part from the U.S. Centers for Disease Control and Prevention.

SAVVY RESOURCES

- AARP "Don't Hesitate—Vaccinate" brochure: Call 1-800-424-3410 or send an e-mail to *member@aarp.org.* Include the fulfillment number with your request (D17438 for the English version, D17449 for Spanish).
- Flu Facts for Everyone: The U.S. Centers for Disease Control and Prevention has more information on preventing and controlling the flu. Call 1-800-232-2522 (English) or 1-800-232-0233 (Spanish), or visit the CDC's Web site at *www.cdc.gov/nip/flu.*
- Focus on the Flu: The National Institute of Allergies and Infectious Diseases (NIAID) has a flu fact sheet, information on flu research and related material: *www.niaid.nih.gov/newsroom/focuson/fluoo/default.htm.*

—Hearing Loss—

CAN YOU HEAR ME? An unsavvy fact about hearing loss is that it affects over 28 million Americans of all ages and is especially prevalent in seniors age 60 and above. Because hearing loss can develop over several years, most people are not aware of the extent of their loss until family or friends bring it to their attention. Even then they might deny that they have difficulty hearing.

SAVVY FACT: Only about 20 percent of Americans who need a hearing aid actually wear one, largely because the devices are perceived as ugly. In fact, there are many extremely discreet ones available.

Hearing-Loss Symptoms

- Difficulty hearing high-pitched sounds, such as women's and children's voices and birds singing.
- Difficulty hearing at public gatherings—concert halls, theaters, houses of worship—where sound sources are far from the listener.
- Difficulty understanding conversations within a group of people or over the telephone.

Three General Types of Hearing Loss

- Sensorineural hearing loss (most common) is characterized by deterioration of the cochlea. Causes are the result of the aging process, exposure to loud noise or a congenital problem.
- Conductive hearing loss occurs when the eardrum, bones and membranes don't properly transmit vibrations to the cochlea. Causes include traumatic head injury and birth defects.
- Mixed hearing loss involves a combination of both conductive and sensorineural hearing loss.

Hearing Options

There are a variety of hearing aid styles and advanced technologies available, depending on individual need and budget. You should contact your hearing-health-care professional for more specific information.

 SAVVY NOTE: Hearing aids are not covered by Medicare.

Hearing-Aid Vanity

Many seniors don't want to wear a hearing aid because they don't like the way it makes them look—but did you know that President Bill Clinton wore a completelyin-the-canal-model hearing aid for most of the last four years of his presidency? Who knew?

SAVVY RESOURCES

For more information on hearing loss and hearing-aid styles and technology, contact a hearing-health-care professional or take advantage of the unlimited amount of information online. Here are a few savvy sites:

- Self Help for Hard of Hearing People (SHHH): *www.hearingloss.org*
- National Campaign for Hearing Health: *www.hearinghealth.net*
- Hearing Loss Web: *www.hearinglossweb.com*
- Healthy Hearing: *www.healthyhearing.com*
- Hearing Planet (online resource on hearing aids, hearing-aid batteries and hearing-aid technology): *www.hearingplanet.com*
- American Speech-Language-Hearing Association: *www.asha.org*
- Sight & Hearing Association: *www.sightandhearing.org*

—Incontinence—

Have you ever heard the expression "I laughed so hard I almost wet my pants"? If so, it probably wasn't from somebody suffering from incontinence. In the United States alone, over 12 million adults have urinary incontinence, most common in women over 50. Today, savvy solutions are available to stop or decrease incontinence in almost everyone—even the very old.

Remember that growing older doesn't necessarily mean your pipes leak! However, age can reduce how much urine your bladder can hold and can make your stream of urine weaker, causing you to feel the urge to urinate more often.

What Causes Incontinence?

Lots of things. Sometimes it's caused by an illness, and when the illness goes away, so does the incontinence. For example, bladder infections and, if you are a woman, infections in the vagina, can cause incontinence for a short while. Being unable to have a bowel movement or taking certain medicines also may make it hard to control your bladder. Other factors that cause urinary leakage are

- A weak bladder.
- Weakening of muscles around the bladder. This happens with women who have had children. Sometimes the weakened muscles cause urine to leak out when you cough, laugh, sneeze or do a particular activity.
- A blocked urinary passageway.
- Damage to the nerves that control the bladder.
- Diseases, such as arthritis, that limit movement.

Solutions

There are many ways to treat incontinence, from exercises to surgery. Ask your doctor what's best for you. Solutions include

- Bladder or habit training: This will train your bladder to hold urine better. Your doctor may ask you to urinate at set times, such as once every hour. The doctor also may tell you not to drink beverages with caffeine. You may want to cut down on how much you drink before going to bed. But drink your usual amount of fluids during the rest of the day.
- Bladder or Pelvic Muscle Exercise (PME): These help make the muscles around the bladder strong so you can hold your urine in your bladder longer. Talk to your doctor about PME options and instructions. The doctor may also suggest using a small device that you put in your vagina or rectum, the low end of the bowel. The device gives a painless electrical pulse that exercises the muscles. This helps the muscles get stronger quicker.
- Drugs: Some common ones are Detrol, Cyctospaz, Ditropan and Levsin. You must have a prescription from a doctor to get these drugs.

- Surgery: Surgery can fix problems such as blocked areas. It also can move the bladder so it doesn't bump into another body part, make the bladder bigger and make weak muscles stronger. A surgeon can also put a small device in the body that acts on nerves to control bladder contractions.
- Tension-free vaginal tape system (TVT): A surgical alternative that has produced quality results (ask your doctor for more information).
- Catheters: If nothing else helps, the doctor may suggest catheters, thin tubes placed in the bladder by a doctor or by the person. They drain the bladder for you, sometimes into an attached plastic bag.

Other Treatments for Women

- Throw-away patch: Sold in drugstores as UroMed or Miniguard patch. The sticky side of the patch goes over the urinary opening. The patch helps hold in urine. It is not good for controlling heavy or even medium leakage.
- Plug: Called the Reliance Urinary Control Insert. This tiny device must be prescribed by a doctor.
- Collagen: This is a protein that your doctor shoots into your body with a needle. Collagen thickens the area around the urethra so that you can control your urine flow better.

This information was obtained in part from the Department of Health and Human Services—Food and Drug Administration. For more information, visit *www.fda.gov*.

SAVVY RESOURCES

- National Association for Continence: 1-800-BLADDER (1-800-252-3337) or *www.nafc.org*
- Simon Foundation for Continence: 1-800-237-4666 or *www.simonfoundation.org*
- National Kidney and Urologic Diseases Information Clearinghouse: *www.niddk.nih.gov/health/urolog/urolog.htm*

— Macular Degeneration —

If you are over 50 years old and you have begun noticing a hazy gray spot in the middle of your vision, develop trouble reading fine print in the newspaper and seeing street signs when you drive, or if big-screen movies don't seem as clear as they once did, **Go Get Checked Out!** You may be experiencing early signs of macular degeneration.

Macular degeneration, also known as age-related macular degeneration (AMD) is a chronic, progressive disease and the leading cause of legal blindness in adults. AMD affects more Americans than cataracts and glaucoma combined. AMD gradually destroys sharp, central vision that's necessary for reading, driving, recognizing people's faces and doing detail work. AMD does not affect side (peripheral) vision, and usually doesn't cause total blindness.

 SAVVY NOTE: In some people, AMD advances so slowly that it will have little effect on their vision as they age. But in others, the disease progresses faster and may lead to a loss of vision in one or both eyes.

Who Gets AMD

The greatest risk factor is age. Studies show that people over age 60 are clearly at greater risk than other age groups. Other risk factors include

- Gender: Women tend to be at greater risk for AMD than men.
- Race: White people are much more likely to lose vision from AMD than black people.
- Smoking: Smoking may increase the risk of AMD.
- Family history: Those with immediate family members who have AMD are at a higher risk.
- Eye color: People with lighter-colored eyes may be at greater risk than those with darker-colored eyes.

AMD Occurs in Two Forms

- Dry AMD: Ninety percent of all people with AMD have this type. In the "dry" type of macular degeneration, the deterioration of the retina is associated with the formation of small yellow deposits, known as *drusen*, under the *macula*, which is the center of the retina. This phenomena leads to a thinning and drying out of the macula. The amount of central vision loss is directly related to the location and amount of retinal thinning caused by the drusen.

- Wet AMD: Although only 10 percent of all people with AMD have this type, it accounts for 90 percent of all blindness from the disease. In the "wet" type of macular degeneration, abnormal blood vessels (known as subretinal neovascularization) grow under the retina and macula. These new blood vessels may then bleed and leak fluid, thereby causing the macula to bulge or lift up, thus distorting or destroying central vision. Under these circumstances, vision loss can be rapid and severe.

Macular degeneration usually develops gradually and painlessly. Symptoms of the disease tend to vary, depending on the type of macular degeneration you develop.

Dry AMD Symptoms

- A gradual increase in the grayness of your vision
- A gradual increase in the haziness of your vision
- A blind spot in the center of your visual field
- Printed words becoming increasingly blurry
- Colors appearing dimmer

Wet AMD Symptoms

- Visual distortions, such as straight lines appearing wavy or crooked
- Sudden, decreased central vision
- A central blind spot

SAVVY NOTE: If you've been diagnosed with wet macular degeneration in one eye, it's likely you'll also develop it in the other eye. If you notice symptoms, see your doctor immediately.

New AMD Treatment

The National Eye Institute is funding a number of research studies to learn what causes AMD and how it can be better treated. For instance, in the Age-Related Eye Diseases Study, researchers are assessing the aging process in the eyes of thousands of older people to discover the earliest signs of AMD. The same study is also evaluating the effects of certain vitamins and minerals in preventing or slowing the progress of AMD.

Current Treatments

- Dry AMD: There are currently no treatments or preventive measures for dry AMD. Low-vision aids and rehabilitation are available to assist patients in coping with vision loss associated with dry AMD.
- Wet AMD: There are only two clinically proven treatments for wet AMD. The first treatment is laser photocoagulation, a surgical procedure involving the application of a hot laser to seal and halt or slow the progression of abnormal blood vessels. The second treatment is photodynamic therapy (PDT), a therapy which uses cold lasers. The therapy was recently approved by the Food and Drug Administration (FDA) in the United States.

SAVVY NOTE: In most cases there is no way to reverse damage caused by AMD, but early detection may help reduce the extent of vision loss. Studies also show that antioxidant supplements like vitamins C, E and beta carotene—as well as zinc or zinc oxide and eating a diet rich in fruits and green vegetables—can help reduce the risk of AMD.

SAVVY RESOURCES

- National Eye Institute: *www.nei.nih.gov*
- Macular Degeneration Foundation: *www.eyesight.org*

- American Macular Degeneration Foundation: *www.macular.org*
- Macular Degeneration Network: *www.macular-degeneration.org*

—Osteoporosis—

Have you ever heard of someone actually breaking a bone by sneezing? For those with severe osteoporosis, it is possible.

Osteoporosis, which means "porous bones," is a disease that causes bones to become weak and brittle. Often bones become so brittle that even mild stresses like bending over, lifting, coughing and even vacuuming the living room can cause a fracture. In most cases, bones weaken when you have low levels of calcium, phosphorous and other minerals in your bones.

 SAVVY FACT: In the United States, one out of every two women, and one in eight men over the age of 50, will have an osteoporosis-related fracture in their lifetime. These fractures usually occur in the spine, hip or wrist.

Signs and Symptoms

Osteoporosis is often called the "silent disease" because bone loss occurs without symptoms. People may not know that they have osteoporosis until their bones become so weak that a sudden strain, bump or fall causes a fracture or a vertebra to collapse. Collapsed vertebrae may initially be felt or seen in the form of severe back pain, loss of height or spinal deformities such as *kyphosis* (stooped posture).

Risk Factors

Early detection is important in osteoporosis. You may be able to slow the disease if you find out you have it, or prevent it if you discover you're likely to develop it. Risk factors include

- Being female
- Thin and/or small frame
- Advanced age
- A family history of osteoporosis
- Postmenopause, including early or surgically induced menopause
- Abnormal absence of menstrual periods (amenorrhea)
- Anorexia nervosa
- A diet low in calcium
- Use of certain medications, such as corticosteroids and anticonvulsants
- Low testosterone levels in men
- An inactive lifestyle, smoking and excessive use of alcohol
- Being Caucasian or Asian, although African Americans and Hispanic Americans are at significant risk as well

Women can lose up to 20 percent of their bone mass in the five to seven years following menopause, making them more susceptible to osteoporosis.

Detection

A specialized test called a bone density test can measure bone density in various sites of the body. A bone density test is fast, simple and painless and can

- Detect osteoporosis before a fracture occurs.
- Predict your chances of fracturing in the future.
- Determine your rate of bone loss and/or monitor the effects of treatment.

Prevention and Treatment

Here are a few savvy tips that can reduce your risk of osteoporosis. If you already have osteoporosis, these tips can also help prevent your bones from becoming weaker, and in some cases, you may even be able to replace bone loss.

- A balanced diet rich in calcium and vitamin D. The higher your peak bone mass, the less likely you'll be to have fractures later in life.

- Weight-bearing exercise can help you build strong bones and slow bone loss.
- Don't smoke, avoid excessive alcohol and limit caffeine intake.
- Hormone replacement therapy (HRT) reduces a woman's risk of osteoporosis during and after menopause. However, the short-term use of HRT to relieve symptoms at the time of menopause does little to prevent fractures in women when they reach 75 to 80 years of age. Talk to your doctor about the risks of taking HRT—coronary heart disease, stroke, blood clots and breast cancer—and which form of HRT would be best for you.

Medications

Although there is no cure for osteoporosis, there are medications that can help prevent, slow or stop its progress. Currently, bisphosphonates (alendronate and risedronate), calcitonin, estrogens, parathyroid hormone and raloxifene are approved by the U.S. Food and Drug Administration (FDA).

Teriparatide, a form of parathyroid hormone, is a newly approved osteoporosis medication. It is the first osteoporosis medication to increase the rate of bone formation in the bone remodeling cycle. Be sure to talk to your doctor about these FDA-approved options. Here is a current list of approved medications and their brand names.

Antiresorptive Medications

- Bisphosphonates: alendronate sodium (brand name Fosamax) and risedronate sodium (brand name Actonel)
- Calcitonin (brand name Miacalcin)
- Estrogen replacement therapy (ERT) and hormone replacement therapy (HRT) (Multiple brand names are available.)
- Raloxifene (brand name Evista)

Bone-Forming Medications

- Parathyroid hormone (brand name Fortéo)

- National Institutes of Health (NIH) Osteoporosis and Related Bone Diseases—
  National Resource Center: *www.osteo.org*
- National Osteoporosis Foundation: *www.nof.org*
- National Women's Health Resource Centers: *www.healthywoman.org*

—Teeth, Gums and Heart—

If your food doesn't seem to taste as good as it used to, don't blame your imagination. It might be your taste buds or nose!

Did you know that along with every other body part, our taste buds and sense of smell can wear out too? It is believed that about 90 percent of our ability to sense flavor is attributed to smell.

- Our sense of smell is at its peak performance when we are in our 30s, 40s and 50s. After age 60, taste and smell begin to gradually decline in most people as a result of the normal aging process.
- We start out in life with about 10,000 taste buds scattered on the tongue. Each area of the tongue can distinguish certain tastes better than others: sweet on the tip, sour on the sides, bitter on the back and salty around the front.

 SAVVY NOTE: Many different types of medications can also affect the ability to taste.

Oral Hygiene and Heart Disease

Studies increasingly show a connection between good gums and good overall health, linking gum disease, otherwise known as periodontal disease, to a variety of systemic problems, including heart disease and stroke.

Early gum disease starts with plaque, the invisible, sticky film of bacteria that sets up house on your tooth enamel. As plaque hardens into tartar, it attracts more than 350 possible varieties of bacteria. As bacteria-rich tartar travels under the gumline, a more advanced gum disease called periodontitis begins (infection of the gum, bone and other tissue surrounding the teeth).

Savvy Study

An accumulating body of evidence suggests that periodontal infection may contribute to arteriosclerotic heart diseases. In a University of Michigan study involving 400 men age 60 and older, researchers found that those suffering from advanced periodontal disease were 4.5 times more likely to have coronary heart disease than those without gum disease.

The reason periodontal disease is so hard on your heart is because people with gum disease tend to have high blood levels of fibrinogen, a molecule that can cause clotting, and C-reactive protein, an inflammatory molecule. Also, a report in the *American Journal of Epidemiology* stated that people with periodontal disease may have higher levels of cholesterol.

The same molecules that affect your heart also can block the blood flow to your brain, causing a stroke. That's not good news, since the National Stroke Association estimates that clots or blockages in arteries account for 80 percent of all strokes.

 NOTE FOR DIABETICS: Researchers have found that uncontrolled diabetes can lead to a higher risk of gum disease, which in turn can make diabetes more problematic, since severe periodontal disease can increase blood sugar.

Tips to Beat Bacteria

With good brushing and flossing habits, and semiannual dental visits, gum disease can usually be prevented or controlled. Here are a few extra tips to keep your mouth and your bloodstream free of plaque:

- Water Pik: The force of the water knocks out the plaque by-products that help bacteria become anaerobic—which are the destructive bacteria. Simply drinking water can also help your gums. Oral bacteria love a dry mouth, which is often caused by smoking, alcohol and normal aging.

- Rubber-tipped stimulator: If you have closely spaced teeth or fillings that catch floss, try using a rubber-tipped stimulator (or soft balsa toothpick). Both are useful in maneuvering around concave, hard-to-reach tooth surfaces like molars.
- Check your medicine: If you take the drug nifedipine for high blood pressure, you may be more susceptible to gum disease. According to the American Academy of Periodontology, 20 to 40 percent of nifedipine users experience enlarged, bleeding gums. Visit the dentist regularly to prevent swelling and infection.

SAVVY RESOURCES

- American Dental Association: *www.ada.org*
- American Academy of Periodontology: *www.perio.org*

— Prostate Checkups —

The motto "Just Do It," coined by Nike, is also a good motto when it comes to prostate checkups.

Prostate cancer is the most common cancer in American men, and it's estimated that by age 50, up to one in four men have some cancerous cells in the prostate gland. By age 80, the ratio increases to one in two. However, unlike other cancers, you're more likely to die *with* prostate cancer than you are *of* it. On average, an American man has about a 30 percent risk of having prostate cancer in his lifetime, but only about a 3 percent risk of dying of the disease.

SAVVY NOTE: One of the biggest fears of many men who have prostate cancer is that their treatment may leave them incontinent or impotent.

What Is the Prostate?

The prostate gland is located behind the pubic bone and in front of the rectum. The prostate's primary function is to produce most of the fluids in semen, including the fluid that nourishes and transports sperm.

Signs and Symptoms of Prostate Cancer

The problem with detecting prostate cancer is that it often doesn't produce any symptoms in its early stages. That's why approximately 40 percent of prostate cancers aren't diagnosed until they've spread beyond the prostate.

 SAVVY NOTE: Prostate cancer symptoms may be similar to *benign prostatic hyperplasia* (BPH), a noncancerous enlargement of the prostate that is a common problem for men in later years.

Signs and Symptoms

- Need to urinate frequently, especially at night
- Difficulty starting to urinate
- Pain or burning with urination
- Weak urine flow and dribbling
- Starting and stopping of your urine flow
- A sensation that your bladder isn't empty
- Blood in your urine
- Painful ejaculation
- General pain in the lower back, hips or upper thighs

Risk Factors

Knowing the risk factors for prostate cancer can help you determine if and when to begin prostate cancer screening. Risk factors include

- Age: As you get older, your risk for prostate cancer increases.
- Race or ethnic group: For reasons that aren't well understood, African-American men are more likely to have prostate cancer than men of any other group in the United States.
- Family history: Studies show that if your father or brother has prostate cancer, your risk for the disease is about twice as great as that of the average male.
- Diet: There is evidence that a high-fat diet may increase prostate cancer risk.

When to Seek Medical Advice

If you have difficulties with urination, see your doctor. Also see your doctor if you experience erectile dysfunction (impotence) that lasts longer than two months or is a recurring problem. These conditions don't always point to prostate cancer, but both can be signs of prostate-related problems.

If you're a man over age 50, you may want to see your doctor to discuss beginning prostate cancer screening. The American Cancer Society and the American Urological Association recommend having an annual blood test to check for prostate-specific antigen (PSA) beginning at age 50, unless you're at high risk of cancer. If you're African American or have a family history of the disease, you may want to begin at age 40. It is also recommended that men have a yearly digital rectal exam (unpleasant but necessary) beginning at age 40.

SAVVY RESOURCES

- American Cancer Society: Prostate cancer resources, including an overview of biology, treatment options and statistics. Call 1-800-ACS-2345 (1-800-227-2345) or visit *www.cancer.org*.
- National Cancer Institute: What you should know about cancer. Visit *www .cancer.gov*.
- Cancer Care: The prostate cancer section of this Web site offers information on treatment options and staging techniques and includes a complete glossary of terms. Log on to *www.cancercareinc.org*.

—Senior Insomnia—

When it comes to getting a good night's sleep, do you ever feel like the old and the restless?

"If only I could get a good night's sleep" is a common complaint, particularly among older Americans. Many seniors have trouble falling asleep and staying asleep, symptoms that can cause daytime fatigue, impair normal functioning and, yes, even cause crankiness. If this is you, keep reading. Maybe this chapter will put you to sleep!

Just Before Bedtime

- If you smoke, stop. Nicotine causes sleeplessness.
- Do not drink coffee or tea, especially in the evening, because caffeine is a stimulant.
- Do not drink soft drinks that contain caffeine (this includes cola and certain lemon-lime soft drinks).
- Do not take naps during the day.
- Avoid eating large meals and snacks before bedtime.
- Avoid any alcoholic drinks. You may feel as if they are relaxing you and helping you to fall asleep, but in reality they produce "rebound insomnia," causing you to wake up shortly after falling asleep, with difficulty going to sleep again.

Sleep Tight

To help eliminate insomnia,

- Exercise.
- Do not watch television or listen to the radio in the bedroom before going to sleep.
- The bedroom should be dark and comfortably cool.
- Try to clear your mind of all distractions and relax.

- Drink some warm milk and take a warm, soothing bath.
- Go to bed at the same time seven nights a week.

 SAVVY FACT: From 12 to 25 percent of healthy seniors report chronic insomnia, but despite their weariness, less than 15 percent receive treatment.

Treatments for Chronic Insomnia

- Diagnosing with your doctor the underlying medical, psychological or behavioral problems.
- Taking sleeping pills, although the long-term use of sleeping pills for chronic insomnia is not recommended. Taking any sleeping pill should be under the supervision of a physician to closely evaluate effectiveness and minimize side effects.
- Trying behavioral techniques to improve sleep, such as relaxation therapy or sleep reconditioning.

Behavioral Approaches

- **Relaxation Therapy:** There are savvy techniques that can reduce or eliminate anxiety and body tension. As a result, the person's mind is able to stop "racing," the muscles can relax and restful sleep can occur.
- **Reconditioning:** The most commonly used treatment that may help with insomnia is to recondition yourself to associate the bed and bedtime with sleep. For most people, this means not using their beds for any activities other than sleep and sex. As part of the reconditioning process, the person is usually advised to go to bed only when sleepy. If unable to fall asleep, the person is told to get up, stay up until sleepy and then return to bed. Throughout this process, the person should avoid naps and wake up and go to bed at the same time each day. Eventually the person's body will be conditioned to associate the bed and bedtime with sleep.

SAVVY RESOURCES

- National Center on Sleep Disorders Research: Call 1-301-435-0199 or visit *www.nhlbi.nih.gov/sleep.*
- American Academy of Sleep Medicine: Call 1-708-492-0930 or visit *www.aasmnet.org.*
- National Sleep Foundation: Call 1-202-347-3471 or visit *www.sleepfoundation.org.*

—Post-Retirement Blues—

Retirement isn't necessarily all it's cracked up to be! In many cases, retirement means that literally overnight, you have no job, no structure, no social interaction with coworkers and lots of free time. Which leaves many seniors (especially men) feeling bored, depressed and without purpose.

 SAVVY NOTE: In today's American society, many men tie their self-esteem and self-worth to their career.

Plan Ahead

Ahh, retirement . . . Finally you have the time to read all those good books, travel, play golf and reconnect with old friends. Sounds great. Maybe not! Experts say that planning ahead is the number one tip for coping with retirement. Although many people plan for retirement financially, few consider the lifestyle changes they will face. Here are some savvy suggestions to help you make the adjustment:

- Phase out of work slowly—work part-time for a while.
- Don't isolate yourself.

- Develop a social network of friends.
- Develop new hobbies and interests.
- Schedule your day to maintain some structure.
- Volunteer.
- Exercise—avoid becoming sedentary.

 SAVVY NOTE: People who do best with retirement have interests and purpose outside of their jobs.

Depression: What to Look For

Here is a list of the most common signs of depression:

- An "empty" feeling, ongoing sadness and anxiety
- Tiredness, lack of energy
- Restlessness, irritability or excessive crying
- Loss of interest or pleasure in everyday activities, including sex
- Insomnia, oversleeping or waking much earlier than usual
- Eating more or less than usual
- Aches and pains that don't go away when treated
- A hard time focusing, remembering or making decisions
- Feeling guilty, helpless, worthless or hopeless
- Thoughts of death or suicide

 SAVVY NOTE: Depression can be tricky to recognize and hard to diagnose; however, the 80–90 percent of those who seek treatment can feel better within a few weeks.

Treatment

Your first step is to visit your doctor or mental health specialist for treatment. Different therapies seem to work for different people. For example, support groups can provide new coping skills or social support if you are dealing with a major life change. Also, don't forget to call on family and friends to help provide support.

Antidepressant drugs also can help. These medications can improve mood, sleep, appetite and concentration. Some antidepressants can take up to 12 weeks before you are aware of any progress. Be sure to first talk to your doctor about this option.

SAVVY FACTS: Depression affects almost 10 percent of the population, or 19 million Americans, in a given year. Two-thirds of those who are depressed never seek treatment. This information was obtained in part from the National Institute on Aging.

SAVVY RESOURCES

- National Institute of Mental Health (NIMH): Call 1-800-421-4211 (for publications) or see their Web site at *www.nimh.nih.gov/publicat/depoldermenu.cfm* for items on depression and older adults.
- National Mental Health Association (NMHA): Call 1-800-969-NMHA (1-800-969-6642) or visit *www.nmha.org*.
- American Association for Geriatric Psychiatry (AAGP): Call 1-301-654-7850 or visit *www.aagpgpa.org*.
- American Psychological Association (APA): Call 1-800-374-2721 or visit *www.apa.org*.

—Men and Grief—

Because women have longer life expectancies than men do, few men expect to outlive their wives. When a man's wife dies, he often loses his best friend, sometimes his only real confidante and his social secretary, as well as the person responsible for many household chores. It is not uncommon for men to realize, perhaps for the first time, how many roles their wives actually played. Grief can be particularly difficult for men who expect—or may be expected by others—to be "strong." A common cultural reminder that "big boys don't cry" can make it hard for men to show emotion and express themselves fully.

Prescriptions as to the best way of grieving for any particular person are impossible, because there is no right or best way to grieve. However, there is evidence that individuals who do not acknowledge the significance of their loss or seek support may prolong the grief process and put themselves at risk for additional stress.

Grief Support—How to Help Others Who Are Grieving

- Be present and willing to listen. Your caring presence and active role is worth volumes.
- Be nonjudgmental.
- Be patient and don't hurry the grief work.
- Provide practical help, like running errands or helping around the house. Do these without taking over.
- Find and recommend a support group that is helpful.
- Find and recommend available programs for community involvement.

SAVVY RESOURCES

- AARP Grief and Loss Programs offer a wide variety of resources and information on bereavement issues for adults of all ages and their families. Services include one-to-one peer outreach support, a grief course, bereavement support groups, informational booklets and brochures, an extensive Web site and interactive online support groups and bulletin boards. For more information, or to find a program in your area, call 1-202-434-2260 or see their Web site at *www.aarp.org/griefandloss*.
- There are many other local organizations that sponsor local bereavement programs. Check into religious organizations such as churches or synagogues, funeral homes, hospices, aging organizations such as the senior centers or Area Agency on Aging, hospitals and mental health or counseling centers.

Suggested Reading

- *On Death and Dying*, by Elisabeth Kübler-Ross
- *When Will I Stop Hurting? Dealing with a Recent Death,* by June Cerza Kolf
- *No Death, No Fear*, by Thich Nhat Hanh and Pritam Singh
- *How to Survive the Loss of a Love,* by Peter McWilliams, Harold H. Bloomfield and Melba Colgrove

—Senior Nutrition—

Many older seniors neglect good eating habits for many reasons. We all need to remember that good nutrition through all stages of life is essential to staying healthy and vital. Studies also show that a good diet in later years helps in reducing the risk of diseases such as osteoporosis, obesity, high blood pressure, heart disease, certain cancers, gastrointestinal problems and chronic undernutrition.

 SAVVY NOTE: Physical activity is also important in maintaining a healthy lifestyle.

Nutritional Neglect

Causes of eating problems for seniors vary from loneliness to lack of desire or cooking skills to financial woes or physical problems.

- Hungry singles: Older people who find themselves single after many years of living with another person may find it difficult to be alone, especially at mealtimes. They may become depressed and lose interest in preparing or eating regular meals, or they may eat only sparingly. For many widowed men who may have left the cooking to their wives, the problem may extend even further: They may not know how to cook and prepare foods.
- Special diets: Many older people, because of chronic medical problems, require special diets—for example, a low-fat, low-cholesterol diet for heart

disease, a low-sodium diet for high blood pressure or a low-calorie diet for weight reduction. Special diets often require extra effort, but older people may instead settle for processed foods that are quick and easy to prepare, such as frozen dinners, canned foods, lunch meats and others that may provide too many calories or contain too much fat and sodium for their needs.

- Physical problems: Some older people may overly restrict foods important to good health because of chewing difficulties and gastrointestinal disturbances, such as constipation, diarrhea and heartburn. Adverse reactions from medications can cause older people to avoid certain foods. Some medications alter the sense of taste, which can adversely affect appetite.

- Money matters: Lack of money is a particular problem among older Americans who may have no income other than Social Security. According to U.S. Census Bureau data for the year 2000, the median annual income for people 65 and over was $13,739. More than 10 percent of people that age had an income below the average poverty level for their age group.

Solutions

Solutions can vary from finding alternative living arrangements to accepting home-delivered meals to using the food label developed by the FDA.

- Food programs: The Older Americans Act provides nutrition and other services that target older people who are in greatest social and economic need. According to the U.S. Administration on Aging, the nutrition programs were set up to address the dietary inadequacy and social isolation among older people. Home-delivered meals and congregate nutrition services are the primary nutrition programs. The congregate-meal program allows seniors to gather at a local site, often the local senior citizen center, school or other public building, or a restaurant, for a meal and other activities, such as games and lectures on nutrition and other topics of interest to older people.

 SAVVY NOTE: While these nutrition programs target low-income seniors, they are available to all older people regardless of income. Also note that in some communities, private organizations sell home-delivered meals. To learn about meal programs in your area, call your Eldercare Locator at 1-800-677-1116.

- Senior assistance: Family members and friends can help out by assisting the older person in taking advantage of the different food programs. Put them in touch with the appropriate agencies or organizations. Looking in occasionally to ensure that the older person is eating adequately, preparing foods and making them available to the older person and joining the older person for meals are all helpful solutions.

Look to the Label

The nutritional value of foods varies greatly, so when you shop, be sure to read the "Nutritional Facts" food label to help select a savvy diet.

This information was obtained in part from the U.S. Food and Drug Administration at *www.fda.gov.*

SAVVY RESOURCES

- National Center for Nutrition: Call Dietetics Consumer Nutrition Hotline at 1-800-366-1655.
- American Dietetic Association: *www.eatright.org.*
- National Cancer Institute's 5 A Day Program: *www.5aday.gov.*

—Second Opinions—

Help yourself to seconds. Second opinions, that is!

Fear of offending the doctor is the number one reason why many seniors don't get another opinion. But good doctors welcome second opinions, and so does Medicare.

You owe it to yourself to know all your options. Medicare offers the following information in their guide "Getting a Second Opinion Before Surgery." Here's what you should know.

How Do I Find a Good Doctor to Get a Second Opinion?

- Do not hesitate to ask your doctor for the name of another doctor to see; most doctors want you to get a second opinion. If you do not want to ask the first doctor, who recommended the surgery, ask another doctor you trust.
- Ask your local medical societies for the names of doctors who treat your illness or injury. Your local library can help you identify these societies.
- Call the Medicare carrier who handles your Medicare Part B bills. Your carrier can give you the names of doctors in your area who accept assignment (accept the Medicare-approved amount as payment in full). This could save you money. To find your carrier, call 1-800-MEDICARE (1-800-633-4227), or look on the Medicare Web site at *www.medicate.gov* under "Helpful Contacts."

How to Get a Second Opinion

When you decide you want a second opinion, ask your doctor's office to send your medical records to the doctor giving the second opinion. That way, you may not have to repeat medical tests. Before you visit the second doctor, call that office and make sure they have your records. During the visit, be sure that the doctor knows what tests you have had and what surgery you want to discuss.

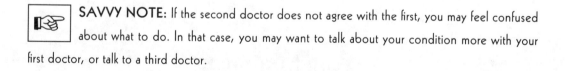 **SAVVY NOTE:** If the second doctor does not agree with the first, you may feel confused about what to do. In that case, you may want to talk about your condition more with your first doctor, or talk to a third doctor.

How Does Medicare Pay for a Second Opinion?

Medicare Part B helps pay for a second opinion just as it helps pay for other doctors' services that are medically necessary.

If you have Medicare Part B and are in the Original Medicare Plan:

- Medicare pays 80 percent of the approved amount for a second opinion. Your share is usually 20 percent of the Medicare-approved amount after you have paid your $100 annual Part B deductible.
- If the second opinion does not agree with the first, Medicare pays 80 percent of the approved amount for a third opinion.

If you are in a Medicare managed care plan (such as an HMO), you have the right to get a second opinion. But some plans will only pay for a second opinion if you first get a referral from your primary care doctor (a referral is a written okay). You must get the second opinion from the doctor named in the referral. If you want to get a second opinion from a doctor who does not belong to your plan, talk to your plan first. Some plans will pay if you do this, but most will not.

For more information, visit *www.medicare.gov* or call 1-800-MEDICARE (1-800-633-4227).

SAVVY RESOURCE

The American Academy of Family Physicians (AAFP): a national nonprofit medical association that provides health and medical information and a national doctor directory. See *www.familydoctor.org*.

—Weight-Training Seniors—

Ever consider lifting weights?

Starting or adding weight training to any exercise program has been shown to boost energy, improve muscle strength and endurance and speed up metabolism for better weight control. Best of all, experts say you are never too old to lift weights. In some nursing homes, residents have traded in their walkers for canes after using weights for their thighs and calves.

Without exercise, muscle mass decreases about 1 percent a year beginning at age 30. Just two 30-minute sessions of weight training a week can push back this process and improve your feeling of overall well-being—not to mention that you'll get stronger! Weight training strengthens bones and helps prevent osteoporosis, reduces the risk for adult-onset diabetes, raises the level of "good" HDL cholesterol and eases arthritis pain. Plus, it affords ease in day-to-day tasks, prevents broken bones, increases endurance, promotes better sleep and, in some cases, eases anxiety and depression.

Getting Started

Before you head for the dumbbells, check with your doctor on advice and approval about your plans, especially if you are on some medications. If you have hypertension, your doctor may run some tests to make sure weight lifting won't elevate your blood pressure.

Where Can I Lift?

After you get the green light, you can decide whether you want to join a gym or lift weights at home. Just be sure to get some advice from a trainer before you begin. Proper technique is vital to the prevention of injuries. The good news is that weight lifting does not require lots of fancy equipment. You can get some hand weights or use resistance bands, canned goods or even plastic milk jugs filled with water. The trick is to do weight-bearing exercises that include several sets of slow repetitions. There are lots of workout videotapes and DVDs available for seniors.

Joining a health club or YMCA offers weight-lifting equipment, socializing and professional guidance. If you are thinking about joining a health club, here are some savvy suggestions from the International Council on Active Aging: Tour the facility. Make sure the exercise equipment has features friendly and comfortable to you, low starting weights and is designed well for your back and knee problems. Check to see if the staff is certified by a nationally recognized fitness organization with CPR training and will provide continuous supervision, screening and assessment of your progress. Also, if the gym has a pool, you can get the same benefits by using water weights.

SAVVY RESOURCES

- National Strength and Conditioning Association: *www.NSCA.org*
- International Council on Aging (ICAA): *www.ICAA.cc*
- American College of Sports Medicine: *www.acsm.org*
- American Association for Active Lifestyles and Fitness: *www.aahperd.org*
- American Council on Exercise: *www.acefitness.org*

— End-of-Life Decisions —

The process of getting one's affairs in order is a very important step! We all have a right to decide what kind and how much care we want or don't want when death is expected. We also have the right to decide where we want to die and whom we wish to care for us.

 SAVVY NOTE: Preparing and making choices now is smart, because someday we won't be able to.

Good Advice

Having direct conversations is the most important thing you can do to plan for the end of life. Decisions about end-of-life medical treatments are deeply personal and should be based on your values and beliefs. Because it is impossible to foresee every type of circumstance or illness, it is essential to think in general about the quality of life that is important to you. After you've decided what you want, have conversations with

- Family and friends. You can then tell them what your preferences are before a crisis occurs. This will help them make informed decisions about your preferences if you're not able to do so.
- Your doctor. You can tell your doctor what's important to you so he or she can honor those wishes while providing medical care.

- Your clergy or spiritual adviser. You can discuss ethical, moral and religious implications of the decisions you are thinking about.

Advance Directives

Advance directive is a general term that describes two kinds of legal documents: living wills and medical powers of attorney. These documents allow a person to give instructions about future medical care should he or she be unable to participate in medical decisions due to serious illness or incapacity. Prepare and sign advance directives that comply with your state law and give to family, friends and doctors.

 SAVVY NOTE: Each state regulates the use of advance directives differently.

The advance directive document should reflect your wishes and appoint someone to make decisions for you if you are unable to do so. The person you appoint should understand and be willing to carry out your wishes. This can be an extremely difficult responsibility, so it's important that you choose that person carefully. The better the person understands your wishes, the more likely he or she will carry them out appropriately. Understanding your wishes also will diminish any guilt and anguish over whether they are doing the right thing. Advance directives include

- A living will or health-care directive, which allows you to document your wishes concerning medical treatments at the end of life.
- A medical power of attorney (or health-care proxy), which allows you to appoint a person you trust as your health-care agent; this person is authorized to make medical decisions on your behalf.

These documents are intended to ensure that your wishes will be known and followed. They will be more helpful and informative if you discuss your wishes with your family, friends and health-care providers as part of your advance care planning.

SAVVY NOTE: These documents become effective only when you can no longer make or communicate decisions for yourself. This information was obtained from Last Acts, Partnership for Caring and AARP.

SAVVY RESOURCES

- AARP—"Planning for Incapacity": This state-specific guide contains all you need to know to make your health-care wishes known and contains forms that comply with your state's laws. Each publication is available for $5. Specify your state, enclose a check or money order payable to LCE, Inc., and send to: Legal Counsel for the Elderly, Inc., P.O. Box 96474, Washington, DC 20090-6474.
- Last Acts—Information for Families: This national coalition offers families information about options at the end of life. Visit *www.lastacts.org*.
- Partnership for Caring: Offers a variety of services, many of which are particularly helpful for older individuals, at *www.partnershipforcaring.org*.
- 5 Wishes: You can order a simplified advance-directives form that is a useful guide to determining your own wishes and is legally valid in most states. Available in English and Spanish for $5. Order at *www.agingwithdignity.org*.
- Medicare: The "Medicare Hospice Benefits" booklet explains Medicare's hospice-care coverage, who is eligible and how to find a hospice program. View it online at *www.medicare.gov* or order it by calling 1-800-633-4227.
- National Hospice and Palliative Care Organization: The NHPCO Web site describes hospice and palliative care and helps people find a program service near them. Visit them at *www.nhpco.org*.

—Funeral Ready—

At some time in our lives, most of us will have to make, or assist in making, funeral arrangements. To help ease funeral shock and surprise, here are some things to know and costs to expect.

Selecting a Funeral Home

This will be your most important decision and should be made very carefully. Choose a funeral home that has a good and honest reputation in the community. If you are not familiar with the funeral homes in your area, ask a relative, friend, hospice, clergy person or doctor for a recommendation.

Also consider meeting with a few different funeral directors in advance to determine with whom you are comfortable and the range of services offered at a cost that meets your needs. The funeral director can help a family create a ceremony that celebrates a life lived, which can be an important part of the healing process. They also can coordinate the services of many community resources that may provide additional support.

☞ **SAVVY TIP:** The Funeral Consumers Alliance (FCA) is a great funeral resource for consumers. They are dedicated to protecting your rights and can assist you with funeral-home shopping, planning and any problems that arise with your chosen funeral home. They also can put you in touch with your local memorial societies. Call 1-800-765-0107 for more information.

What Kind of Funeral?

Every family is different, and not everyone wants the same type of funeral. Funeral practices are influenced by religious and cultural traditions as well as costs and personal preferences. These factors help determine whether the funeral will be elaborate or simple, public or private, religious or secular, and where it will be held. They also influence whether the body will be present at the funeral, if there will be a viewing or visitation, and if so, whether the casket will be open or closed and whether the remains will be buried or cremated.

Memorial Service

Much like a funeral, a memorial service celebrates the life of the deceased. The only difference is that there is no body present. In recent years, more and more people choose memorials, especially for those whose loved ones have been cremated. The advantage of a memorial service is the cost—no embalming, no casket, no cemetery fee and no headstone.

Funeral Cost

Funeral costs will vary depending on the services and merchandise selections made. Under the Federal Trade Commission regulation, funeral directors are required to provide a general price list of itemized costs of all options offered by their funeral home at the time arrangements are first discussed, or over the telephone if a consumer inquires about the costs. Be sure to ask for this "funeral rule" price list and resist pressure to buy any services you don't want. Here is the national average cost list of commonly selected (funeral only) services based on the most recent survey by the National Funeral Directors Association.

Professional service charges	$1,213
Embalming and cosmetology	570
Visitation/viewing	275
Funeral at funeral home	350
Transfer of remains to funeral home	154
Hearse (local) and service car/van	270
Acknowledgment cards	18
Casket	2,330
Funeral Total	**$5,180**

Note: These prices do not include cemetery charges, such as grave or plot space, vaults, opening/closing grave, crypts/mausoleum, monument or marker. These items are usually not purchased through the funeral home. Cemetery cost will vary greatly, but you can expect to pay on an average between $1,000 and $4,000 depending on what you choose and where you are buried.

Preplanning

Most American funeral homes offer prearrangement options to families. Among the biggest reasons consumers prearrange is the peace of mind that comes with knowing that a spouse or child will not be left with making important decisions at a stressful time. Preplanning also ensures the family that their loved one's final wishes will be met.

Cremation Option

Cremation has become a widespread practice in many parts of the world. The cremation rate in the United States in now around 26 percent, but in Canada it's 45 percent and in England and Japan, where cemetery space is at a premium, the cremation rate is close to 90 percent. One of the biggest advantages of cremation is that it is cheaper than a funeral and cemetery burial. With cremation, no casket is needed and one can usually be rented for a visitation service, if desired. Embalming isn't required either, no matter what the funeral home may try to tell you—or sell you. And then there's the expense of the grave site, which can be avoided. The actual costs will vary, of course, depending on factors such as transportation, permits, urns and more, but cremation can save thousands. In some cases, the total cost can be under $500.

Preplanning Can Be a Good Thing

There are many advantages to planning your funeral, such as

- Choosing the type of funeral service you desire.
- Saving your survivors from making choices during the stress of bereavement.
- Being able to comparison shop at available mortuaries.
- Being able to make knowledgeable decisions.
- Stimulating family discussion, sharing and decision making on an important topic.

 SAVVY NOTE: Preplanning does not mean prepaying. If prepaying is required, keep on reading.

FUNERAL PREPAY

"Pay now—die later" is a growing trend for many in the funeral industry! It's estimated that 9 to 11 million Americans have already bought some $21 billion worth of prepaid funerals. But buyer beware! There are a number of pitfalls and options you need to know about before you can truly rest in peace.

Prepay with Caution

There are lots of salespeople in the funeral industry who will try to convince you to pay in advance for funeral and/or burial arrangements. But this may not be the best choice. Consider the following:

- The cost of paying in advance as compared to paying at death, taking into account any lost investment income from the money spent.
- The possibility that the funeral home may go out of business or be bought out by another company.
- The possibility of moving to another area of the state or country. Will the funeral plan travel with you?
- That you must tell someone that you have prepaid and exactly what you paid for. Make certain at least two people have copies of the paperwork and are prepared to make sure the contract is fulfilled.
- Whether the prices are "locked in" or can change. Money paid today may not cover future inflated funeral costs, resulting in possible substitution of less expensive merchandise or additional funding from survivors (just what you tried to avoid).
- Whether prices are guaranteed if death occurs outside your local area.
- Whether the price is reasonable and the package of services is complete. Getting a detailed list of what is included and comparison shopping will help answer this question.

Financing a Funeral

Rather than giving your money to a funeral home, consider setting up a bank account or trust which will pay upon death to the person you designate to take care of your final arrangements. One good option to consider is the Totten Trust. This is an individual trust or savings plan earmarked for one's funeral. With a Totten Trust, you control the account and can withdraw from it at any time. Usually a sum of money equal to today's funeral costs is deposited in a passbook, certificate of deposit (CD) or money market account, payable to a beneficiary of your choice. This fund will be available immediately at the time of your death without the delay of probate.

Shop Before You Drop

Comparison shopping is a good thing when making funeral arrangements. The costs of such items as caskets or "professional services" will vary dramatically from mortuary to mortuary. Compare prices from at least three places.

SAVVY TIPS: If you are not sure what is included in professional services, be sure to ask. Also there are many companies who sell caskets online for huge discounts. For more information visit the National Casket Retailer's Association Web site at *www.casketstores.com*.

SAVVY RESOURCES

- Funeral Consumers Alliance (FCA): a nonprofit, educational organization that supports funeral consumer protection. Call 1-800-765-0107 or visit *www.funerals.org*. FCA also offers a helpful 20-page booklet called "Before I Go, You Should Know," available for $10.
- Cremation.com: This Web site has a religious issues section, and provides cremation information and assistance in locating a provider for cremation services. Visit *www.cremation.com*.
- Funeral Service Consumer Assistance Program (FSCAP): a nonprofit consumer service created to help consumers in matters involving funeral service. Call 1-800-662-7666 or visit *www.funeralservicefoundation.org* and click on "Consumer Assistance."

- *When Death Occurs*, by John Reigle: A practical consumer's guide on funerals, memorials, burial, cremation and body donation. Cost: $19.95. Call 1-989-370-7116 or visit *www.whendeathoccurs.com*.
- National Funeral Directors Association: Call 1-800-228-6332 or log on at *www.nfda.org/resources*.

MEDICARE AND MORE

MANY SENIORS THINK THAT MEDICARE IS A COMPLICATED TOPIC. IT IS! And you really can't get around it, but in this section you'll learn the need-to-know basics that can help you better understand the ABCs of this program. Beginning with the basics of Medicare Part A and B, we also cover the new Medicare prescription drug benefit, Medicare Choice, Medigap supplemental insurance, Medicaid and nursing-home care, hospice and Medicare and more, as well as tell you where to get more help on these issues.

How about some help with your overpriced prescription medications? Beginning on page 171, *The Savvy Senior*, with the help of the Medicare Rights Center, provides you with a complete list of available discount options, programs and Web sites that might be able to help cut your prescription costs.

—The Basics of Medicare—

We all know what Medicare is, but do we actually understand it?

The Medicare program is a federal health-insurance program for people 65 years of age and older, and certain disabled people under age 65. To be eligible for Medicare you must be a U.S. citizen or permanent resident of the United States who is eligible to receive benefits from Social Security.

Medicare Part A

Medicare has two parts, Part A and Part B. Medicare Part A (hospital insurance) helps pay for inpatient hospital care, inpatient care in a skilled-nursing facility, home health care and hospice care.

 SAVVY NOTE: The Medicare Part A deductible for inpatient hospital care per benefit period is $876 in 2004, and increases every year. The term "benefit period" is a period of time that begins the day you enter the hospital or skilled-nursing facility and continues until you have been out for 60 consecutive days.

Medicare Part B

Medicare Part B (medical insurance) helps pay for doctor services, some preventive services, outpatient hospital and emergency room services, medical equipment and supplies, laboratory services, X-rays, physical therapy, ambulance services and a number of other medical services and supplies that are not covered by Medicare Part A.

Medicare Cost

Medicare Part A is free, but Medicare Part B is a voluntary program (which may be refused) and costs $66.60 a month in 2004. Medicare Part B pays 80 percent of services covered under Part B after a $100 deductible.

 SAVVY NOTE: In 2005 the Medicare Part B deductible will increase to $110 and rise yearly afterward.

Medicare and Nursing-Home Care

To qualify for Medicare nursing-home benefits you must have been an inpatient in a hospital for at least three days and discharged no more than 30 days before entering the nursing home. A physician must also "certify" that you require skilled-nursing care or rehabilitation that can only be provided in a skilled-nursing facility. If you qualify, Medicare pays 100 percent of the charges for the first 20 days. From day 21 to day 100, the patient must pay $109.50/day while Medicare picks up the difference. After day 100, Medicare pays nothing.

What Medicare Does Not Cover

Other medical services and products not covered by Medicare include outpatient prescription drugs, private hospital room, hospital telephone and TV, routine physicals, most dental care, dentures, routine foot care, hearing aids, routine eye care, acupuncture, health care outside the United States and cosmetic surgery.

 SAVVY TIP: For detailed information on what Medicare covers in your area, visit the Medicare Coverage Database at *www.cms.hhs.gov/med*.

Supplemental Health Care

It is savvy advice to purchase a Medicare supplemental or Medigap policy (see Medigap Insurance, page 155) at the time you apply for Medicare services. This type of policy (regulated by state insurance departments and sold by many companies) is designed to fill in the health-care expenses not covered by Medicare. Every new Medicare recipient who is age 65 or older has a guaranteed right to buy a Medicare supplement policy. A company cannot reject you for any policy it sells, nor can it charge you more than anyone else your age. You must, however, purchase the supplement policy within the six-month window after enrolling in Medicare Part B for the first time. If you apply for a policy after your six-month period, some companies may refuse coverage for health reasons.

 SAVVY NOTE: If you are age 65 and not eligible for the free Medicare Part A, you can still get it, but you'll have to pay a steep monthly premium. Medicare Part B is also available (for $66.60/month in 2004). You can enroll in Part B without getting Part A, but if you choose to enroll in Part A you are required to get Part B too. For more detailed information on Medicare, visit *www.medicare.gov* or call 1-800-633-4227 and order the *Medicare & You* handbook. This is a free publication that provides great information and is updated every year.

—The New Medicare Prescription Drug Benefit—

HOW WILL IT AFFECT YOU?

Containing the most extensive changes to the Medicare program since it began in 1965, the new $400 billion prescription drug benefit will offer some help to its beneficiaries, but how much?

Currently, Medicare covers 40 million elderly and disabled Americans. Of those, more than 10 million are without any form of prescription drug coverage and 14 million are low-income seniors. Here's a preview of what you can expect from the new prescription drug benefit, which will be known as Medicare Part D. This information was obtained in part from the Department of Health and Human Services and the Associated Press.

Interim Discount Card

From June 2004 through 2005 a discount card will be available for Medicare recipients to buy for $30. This card will reduce drug costs by 15 percent or more.

Medicare Drug Benefit

Beginning in 2006, Medicare beneficiaries can sign up for a drug plan or join a private health plan that offers drug coverage. Under the Medicare plan, you will be charged a $35-a-month premium per person, or $420 a year. After you pay a $250 deductible, insurance will cover 75 percent of your drug costs up to $2,250. You would thus pay up to $750 out of pocket. (The $250 deductible plus 25 percent of the cost from $251 to $2,250, or $500.) This does not count your $420-a-year premium.

Coverage Gap

After you have incurred $2,250 in total drug costs, Medicare will pay nothing more until you have paid $3,600 out of pocket, meaning you would have to pay $2,850 more out of pocket in addition to the $750 already paid. This does not count your $420 annual premium.

Catastrophic Coverage

When your out-of-pocket spending reaches $3,600, you will pay 5 percent of the cost of each prescription. Medicare pays the other 95 percent.

SAVINGS CHART

The following chart shows how more than 25 million seniors, mostly middle income, will fare under the 2006 Medicare prescription drug benefit. Another 14.1 million lower-income seniors, including those eligible for Medicaid, will fare better.

Drug Cost (One Year)	You Pay	You Save
$1,000	$857.50	$142.50 or 14%
$1,500	$982.50	$517.50 or 34%
$2,000	$1,107.50	$892.50 or 45%
$2,500	$1,420.00	$1,080.00 or 43%
$3,000	$1,920.00	$1,080.00 or 36%
$5,000	$3,920.00	$1,080.00 or 22%
$10,000	$4,265.00	$5,735.00 or 57%

Note: *You Pay* is your total out-of-pocket expense, which includes the $420 annual premium, the $250 deductible and the 25 percent additional costs based on a complex formula. Catastrophic coverage is also figured into the formula.

 SAVVY TIP: You will have to spend at least $810 a year on prescription drugs to benefit from the Medicare prescription drug benefit. That's because you'll spend more on your premium ($420), deductible ($250) and 25 percent out-of-pocket drug costs than you'll get back in Medicare coverage.

Limited-Income Subsidies

In 2004 and 2005, low-income recipients earning less than $12,124 a year, or $16,363 for married couples, will receive an annual subsidy of $600 credited to their drug discount card to help defray drug costs.

Beginning in 2006, people eligible for Medicaid and Medicare will pay no premium or deductible and have no gap in coverage. They will pay $1 per prescription for generics and $3 for brand names. Copays are waived for those in nursing homes.

Members with limited income below the federal poverty line—around $13,000 for individuals and $17,600 for couples, with assets under $6,000 for individuals and $9,000 for couples—will be entitled to different benefits: They will pay no premium or deductible, nor will they face a gap in coverage. For generic drugs there is a $2 copay and a $5 copay for all other drugs, up to the out-of-pocket limit.

Members with savings and incomes below the federal poverty level—between $13,000 and $14,400 for individuals and $17,600 and $19,500 for couples, with assets under $10,000 for individuals and $20,000 for couples—will be entitled to the following benefits: a monthly premium based on a sliding scale; a $50 deductible; no gap in coverage; coinsurance of 15 percent, up to the out-of-pocket limit; and copayments of either $2 or $5 after reaching the out-of-pocket expense limit.

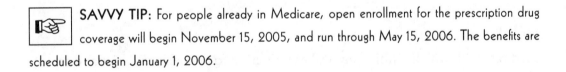 **SAVVY TIP:** For people already in Medicare, open enrollment for the prescription drug coverage will begin November 15, 2005, and run through May 15, 2006. The benefits are scheduled to begin January 1, 2006.

Retiree Coverage

Tax-free subsidies, worth more than $70 billion over 10 years, will be provided to employers who maintain drug coverage for retirees once the Medicare drug benefit begins in 2006. But some employers may still drop their drug coverage. You'll need to check!

Generic Drugs

The ability of pharmaceutical companies to block cheaper equivalents will be limited, which should help speed generic drugs to the market.

Drugs from Canada

The ban on importing prescription drugs from abroad will be maintained, but such drugs will be allowed from Canada if the Department of Health and Human Services certifies their safety, which the department has thus far refused to do. Also, a study of safety issues will be authorized.

OTHER CHANGES TO MEDICARE
Doctors' Services and Other Out-of-Hospital
(Part B) Coverage

Premium

People with incomes greater than $80,000 a year will pay a larger Part B premium for doctors' services and outpatient care. The size of the premium will increase with income, roughly tripling for people with an income over $200,000.

Deductible

The deductible will rise from $100 to $110 in 2005, and thereafter will be indexed to the growth in Part B spending.

New Benefits

Medicare will cover an initial physical examination for new beneficiaries and screening for diabetes and cardiovascular disease. It will provide benefits for coordinated care for people with chronic illnesses and will increase payments for doctors administering mammograms to encourage their use.

Health Savings Accounts

People under age 65 with high-deductible health-insurance policies—$1,000 a year for individuals, $2,000 for couples—will be allowed to shelter income from taxes by depositing a certain amount of money in health savings accounts. Investors will receive a tax deduction and pay no taxes on the investment and earnings upon withdrawal, provided the money is used for health expenses; otherwise, a 10 percent penalty will apply. Talk to your health-insurance provider for more information on health savings accounts.

Rural Health

Medicare payments to rural hospitals and doctors, among others, will be increased by $25 billion over 10 years.

Hospital Payments

Hospitals can avoid future cuts in payments by submitting data on the quality of care to the federal agency that runs the Medicare program. At the same time, payments through Medicaid to hospitals that serve a large number of disadvantaged patients will increase. An 18-month pause in the development of new specialty hospitals will be imposed, and there will be a limit on the expansion of existing ones.

Physician Payments

Doctors will receive increases of 1.5 percent per year in Medicare payments for 2004 and 2005.

Home Health Care

Payments to home health agencies will be cut, but copayments from patients will not be required.

The New Role of Private Companies

Private firms will administer the new drug benefit on a regional basis. It will provide $12 billion in subsidies to private insurers that choose to offer basic health insurance. Those insurers include preferred provider organizations (PPOs), which encourage use of certain doctors but allow patients to go elsewhere if they pay extra, and private fee-for-service plans, which allow patients to see any doctor.

SAVVY NOTE: Medicare Advantage will replace Medicare + Choice, the current managed-care program, in 2006.

Medigap Change

Starting in 2006, Medicare beneficiaries who enroll in the new drug plan will not be allowed to buy Medigap policies to help defray drug costs. However, those people who choose to forgo the new Medicare drug benefit can renew their Medigap drug benefit policy.

2010 Competition

Starting in 2010, Medicare will test competition between private health plans and the government. The experiment will involve up to 2 million seniors in six metropolitan areas for six years. Affected seniors might have to pay 5 percent more a year to stay in Medicare if private insurers offer cheaper coverage.

 SAVVY TIP: To help you better understand the new Medicare reform changes and prescription drug benefit, call your local health-insurance counseling program (SHIP). Call 1-800-633-4227 to get your local number. Also see Health-Insurance Help on page 164.

—Medicare + Choice Plan—

Are you ready to experience the Medicare alphabet in a whole new way? There is Medicare Part A, Part B, and now C, also called the Medicare + Choice Plan.

Congress created the Medicare + Choice program to provide you with more choices and sometimes extra benefits by letting private companies offer you your Medicare benefits.

Original Medicare Plan

It's important to be clear on the *Original Medicare Plan*, also known as Medicare Part A and B, because this will affect your Medicare + Choices. Simply put, Part A is the hospital insurance, and Part B, referred to as medical insurance, helps pay for doctor visits or medical equipment that you may need. At age 65 (if eligible), you automatically get Part A when you sign up for Medicare, although Part B is optional. If you sign up for Part B, you pay a monthly premium, but if you don't, you won't be eligible for Medicare + C.

Think C, for Choice

Medicare + Choice is offered by private companies that contract with the Medicare program to offer services. It is still part of Medicare, and depending on your circumstances and where you live, it certainly may be worth a look.

Medicare + Choice plans include

- Medicare managed-care plans (like HMOs), and
- Medicare private fee-for-service plans.

The real advantage of Medicare + Choice is that it goes beyond traditional Medicare coverage. It may pay for a general annual physical, for example, or for prescription drugs, which are not covered under traditional Medicare (A and B). And while there is a monthly premium, there may be lower out-of-pocket costs with such things as deductibles and copays. But Medicare + Choice options are not offered everywhere, and while there are some limited fee-for-service packages available, most Medicare + Choice programs are managed-care plans like HMOs, PPOs, PSOs and PFFs, in which the patient/member agrees to receive care from specific doctors, hospitals and others—called a network—in exchange for reduced overall health-care costs. That's the part of the plan that many people don't like, especially if it means they can no longer continue to see their own doctor or use the hospital of their choice. But your doctor may already participate in a plan for your area. You'll have to check.

SAVVY NOTE: In 2006, Medicare + Choice will be replaced by Medicare Advantage— a comprehensive care program that will combine health coverage with the drug benefit.

The Best Choice for You

How you get your Medicare health benefits affects many things—like cost, extra benefits, doctor choice, convenience and quality. They all are important, but some may be more important to you than others. You need to look at what plans are available in your area, what each plan offers, and make the best choice.

Your choice will affect:

- Cost: What will my out-of-pocket costs be?
- Benefits: Do I need extra benefits and services, like prescription drugs, eye exams, hearing aids or routine physical exams?
- Doctor Choice: Can I see the doctor(s) I want to see? Do I need a referral to see a specialist?
- Convenience: Where are the doctors' offices and what are their hours? Is there paperwork? Do I have to file claims myself? Is there a telephone hotline for medical advice from a nurse or other medical staff?

SAVVY NOTE: If you join Medicare + C, you leave the Medicare program altogether. The insurance company that runs the plan you choose gets a monthly payment from Medicare on your behalf, and has complete authority to approve or refuse your medical coverage.

Switching Medicare Coverage

If you don't like Medicare + Choice, you can always enroll back in the original Medicare (Parts A and B) plan. But keep in mind that if you return to Medicare after the first year following your initial Medicare eligibility, you may find that not all Medigap supplemental policies will accept you. And you may be able to join another managed-care plan only during the open enrollment period.

- Medicare: For more information on Medicare + Choice plans available in your area, visit *www.medicare.gov/mphcompare/home.asp*. You can research them by state or even by zip code.

- Your State Health Insurance Program (SHIP): They provide free one-on-one counseling and assistance via telephone on a wide range of Medicare issues and can help you make informed choices about Medicare coverage options, including the Medicare + Choice options. To locate your local SHIP office, call 1-800-633-4227 or visit *www.medicare.gov/Contacts/Related/Ships.asp*.

— Medicare Enrollment —

If you are nearing age 65, don't forget to enroll with Medicare. Here's what you should know.

Eligibility

Generally, you are eligible for Medicare if you or your spouse worked for at least 10 years in Medicare-covered employment and you are 65 years old and a citizen or permanent resident of the United States. You might also qualify for coverage if you are a younger person with a disability.

Remember That Medicare Has Two Parts

- Medicare Part A (hospital insurance), which helps pay for care in a hospital and skilled-nursing facility, home health care and hospice care. Most people do not have to pay for Medicare Part A.

- Medicare Part B (medical insurance), which helps pay for doctors, outpatient hospital care and other medical services. Most people pay a monthly premium ($66.60 in 2004) for Medicare Part B.

Medicare Enrollment

How do you sign up for Medicare Parts A and B if you are close to age 65 and get or can get Social Security benefits?

- If you already get Social Security benefits: You will not need to do anything. Simple enough! You will be automatically enrolled in Medicare Part A and Part B effective the month you turn 65. Your Medicare card will be mailed to you about three months before your 65th birthday. If you do not want Medicare Part B coverage (because, for example, you are still working and are covered by an employment-related plan), follow the instructions on the form that comes with the card.

 SAVVY TIP: If you do not receive your Medicare card in the mail within a month of your 65th birthday, call 1-800-772-1213.

- If you want to apply for both Social Security and Medicare: If you are close to age 65 and not yet getting Social Security benefits or Medicare, you will need to actually apply, and you can do both at the same time if you choose. To make sure that your Medicare Part B coverage start date is not delayed, you should apply three months before the month you turn 65. This is the beginning of your seven-month Initial Enrollment Period. If you wait until you are 65, or in the last three months of your Initial Enrollment Period, your Medicare Part B coverage start date will be delayed. To apply, you can call or visit your local Social Security office or call Social Security at 1-800-772-1213. You can also apply online at *www.socialsecurity.gov* if you meet certain rules.

- If you do not yet get Social Security benefits: If you are close to age 65 and not getting Social Security benefits, you must apply for Medicare. Again, you should apply three months before the month you turn 65. If you wait until you are 65, or in the last three months of your Initial Enrollment Period, your Medicare Part B coverage start date will be delayed.

To apply, you can call or visit your local Social Security office or call Social Security at 1-800-772-1213. You currently cannot apply for Medicare solely online (using the Internet).

Don't Delay

Signing up on time is important for two reasons. First, it will ensure that your coverage begins as soon as you are eligible, on your 65th birthday. Second, if you wait more than three months after your 65th birthday to enroll, you will not be allowed to enroll in Part B until the following General Enrollment Period (between January 1 and March 31), and your eligibility will not begin until July 1 of that year. Also, your Medicare Part B premium may go up 10 percent for each 12-month period that you could have had Medicare Part B but did not take it.

Working with Health-Coverage Exception

If you are age 65, you may elect to delay enrolling in Part B (medical insurance) without paying higher premiums if you or your spouse are working and have group health-plan coverage through your or your spouse's employer or union (employer must have 20 or more employees). If this is the case, you may sign up for Medicare Part B during what is called a *Special Enrollment Period.*

The Special Enrollment Period is

- Any time you are still covered by the employer or union group health plan through your or your spouse's current or active employment.
- During the eight months following the month the employer or union group health plan coverage ends, or when the employment ends (whichever is first).

SAVVY NOTES: If you are disabled and working (or you have coverage from a working family member), the Special Enrollment Period rules also apply. Also, if you do not enroll in Medicare Part B during your Special Enrollment Period, you'll have to wait until the next General Enrollment Period, which is January 1 through March 31 of each year. This could result in a 10 percent increase on your Medicare Part B premium.

—Appealing Medicare—

Whether you are covered by the Original Medicare Plan, a Medicare managed-care plan or a private fee-for-service plan, you have the right to appeal a Medicare claim that has been denied in part or in whole. Unfortunately, the Medicare appeal procedure can be a little confusing.

 SAVVY FACT: Claimants who file Medicare appeals are successful more than 50 percent of the time.

The appeals process for the Original Medicare Plan varies a little between Part A and Part B. Here's the general breakdown:

Part A

The Part A appeals process consists of four different levels of appeal. Each level of appeal has its own requirements regarding the minimum dollar amount that can be appealed and the time limit for appealing the denial.

1. Reconsideration

A Medicare beneficiary has the right to appeal an initial claim denial, regardless of the dollar amount in question. The best place to start is with the Medicare Summary Notice that you receive in the mail. This statement should list all of the services, supplies and equipment billed to Medicare. This notice should also tell you why any specific claim was denied. Identify the items you are disputing and the reason why, sign the form and provide your telephone number and send it to the address on the form. You will want to include all the information you can from the doctor or hospital about why the disputed service was medically necessary. You must file a written appeal within 120 days of the initial denial. You can also use the form CMS 2649 to file.

2. Hearing

If the initial appeal is denied, and the dollar amount of the denial is $100 or more, the Medicare beneficiary has the right to request a hearing with an Administrative Law Judge (ALJ). The request must be made within 60 days of the reconsideration denial, using form CMS 5011A-U6.

3. Appeals Council Review

If the claim remains denied following a hearing by an Administrative Law Judge, the Medicare beneficiary has the right to submit an appeal to the Appeals Council Review panel in Washington, D.C. The request must be made within 60 days of the decision by the hearing board, using form HA-520.

4. Civil Litigation

If the appeal is denied following review by the Appeals Council, the Medicare beneficiary has the right to judicial review of the denial in federal court. The request must be made within 60 days of the decision by the Appeals Council. There is no special form to use. The beneficiary must file a civil action in federal district court. The dollar amount of the denial in question must be $1,000 or more.

Part B

The Part B appeals process consists of five different levels of appeal. Each level of appeal has its own requirements regarding the minimum dollar amount that can be appealed and the time limit for appealing the denial.

1. Carrier Review

A Medicare beneficiary has the right to appeal an initial claim denial, regardless of the dollar amount in question. Again, the best place to start is with your Medicare Summary Notice that you receive in the mail. This statement should list all of the services, supplies and equipment billed to Medicare. This notice should also tell you why any specific claim was denied. Identify the items you are disputing and the reason why, sign the form and provide your telephone number and send it to the address on the form. You will want to include all the information you can from the doctor or hospital about why the disputed service was medically necessary. You must file a written appeal within 120 days of the initial denial. You can also use form CMS 1964.

2. Carrier Hearing

If the initial appeal is denied, and the dollar amount of the denial is $100 or more, the Medicare beneficiary has the right to request a hearing. The request must be made to the Medicare claim payer within six months of the denial by the review committee, using form CMS 1965.

3. Administrative Law Judge

If the claim remains denied following a hearing, the Medicare beneficiary has the right to have the claim reviewed by an Administrative Law Judge. The request must be made within 60 days of the decision by the hearing board. The form to be used is CMS-5011B. The dollar amount of the denial must be $100 or more.

4. Appeals Council Review

If the appeal is denied by the Administrative Law Judge, the Medicare beneficiary has the right to have the claim reviewed by the Appeals Council. The request must be made within 60 days of the decision by the Administrative Law Judge. The form to be used is HA-520.

5. U.S. District Court

If the appeal is denied by the Appeals Council, the Medicare beneficiary can have the claim reviewed by the U.S. district court. The request must be made within 60 days of the decision by the Appeals Council. The dollar amount of the denial in question must be $1,000 or more.

Managed Care and Fee-for-Service Appeals

Seniors in Medicare managed-care plans or private fee-for-service plans have similar rights to those in the Original Medicare Plan. These plans must tell you in writing how you can appeal a denied claim. After you file an appeal, the individual plan will review your appeal and make a decision. If your claim remains denied, an independent organization that works for Medicare, not the plan, will review your appeal.

Ambulance Extra

Many people ask about Medicare and ambulance service. Medicare covers ambulance transportation only when the condition of the patient is such that any other method of transportation is inadvisable, and then it will pay for transportation only to the nearest hospital where services are available.

Medicare will pay for the transportation to another facility only if there is a medical reason for doing so; it will not pay for an ambulance if the trip is determined to be for "convenience." Also, Medicare does not pay for ambulance transportation to a doctor's office, and it will pay to transport a person home from the hospital only if that person is confined to a bed and unable to tolerate any other method of transportation.

SAVVY RESOURCES

- Medicare: offers detailed information on what Medicare covers, as well as the appeals process. You can download forms from the Internet at *www.medicare.gov*.
- State Health Insurance Program (SHIP): Each state offers free health-insurance counseling. They can help you understand your bills and file Medicare appeals. To locate your local SHIP, call Medicare at 1-800-633-4227 or visit *www.medicare.gov/Contacts/Related/Ships.asp*.

— Medigap Insurance —

If Medicare and Medicaid aren't enough to confuse you, along comes Medigap!

What Is It?

Medigap (also known as Medicare Supplement Insurance) is a health-insurance policy sold by private insurance companies to fill the "gaps" (expenses not covered by Medicare) in Original Medicare Plan coverage.

There are 10 standardized Medigap plans, "A" through "J." Each plan has a different set of standardized benefits. Plan A offers the least amount of benefits and Plan J offers the most.

 SAVVY NOTE: Massachusetts, Minnesota and Wisconsin residents have different types of Medigap plans.

When you buy a Medigap policy, you pay a premium to the insurance company. As long as you pay your premium, a policy bought after 1990 is automatically renewed each year. This means that your coverage continues year after year.

 SAVVY NOTE: Medigap policies work only with the Original Medicare Plan.

Can I Keep Seeing My Same Doctor If I Buy a Medigap Policy?

In most cases, yes! If you are in the Original Medicare Plan and you have a Medigap policy, you can go to any doctor, hospital or other health-care provider who accepts Medicare. But if you have the type of Medigap policy called Medicare SELECT, you must use specific hospitals and, in some cases, doctors (except in an emergency) to get your full insurance benefits.

When to Buy a Medigap Policy

The best time to buy a Medigap policy is during your Medigap open enrollment period, which lasts for six months and begins on the first day of the month in which you turn age 65 and are enrolled in Medicare Part B.

During this period, an insurance company cannot deny you insurance coverage, place conditions on a policy (like making you wait for coverage to start) or change the price of a policy because of past or present health problems. They must also shorten the waiting period for preexisting conditions.

SAVVY NOTE: Many states provide extra Medigap protections in addition to those listed here. In these states, residents who are enrolled in Medicare Parts A and B may be allowed to purchase Medigap policies at any time throughout the year. For information on your state's regulations, contact your State Health Insurance Program. To get the number, call 1-800-633-4227 or visit *www.medicare.gov/Contacts/Related/Ships.asp*.

Medigap Shopping

Only you can decide if a Medigap policy is the right kind of health-insurance coverage for you. If you decide to buy a Medigap policy, shop carefully. Look for a policy that you can afford and that gives you the coverage you need most. As you shop, keep in mind that insurance companies may charge different amounts for the same Medigap policy.

Other Medigap Considerations

- Contact your state insurance department to find out which insurance companies in your state offer the plan you've chosen and compare the premiums they charge. Also, check the method of rating (pricing). Policies are rated three ways: *attained-age, issue-age* and *community-rated*. You might want to look for community-rated and issue-age-rated policies. They may be the best buy because even though they may cost you more at age 65, they'll cost you less as you get older.
- Check to see whether the Medigap insurer you choose has arranged for Medicare to file your Medigap claims automatically. Automatic claims filing can save you time and headaches.

SAVVY RESOURCES

- Medicare Help Line: They can answer your questions and provide up-to-date information about Medicare, managed-care plans and private fee-for-service plans in your area. Call 1-800-633-4227 or see *www.medicare.gov*.
- State Health Insurance Program (SHIP) offers free one-on-one counseling. To contact your local SHIP office, call Medicare at 1-800-633-4227 or visit *www.medicare.gov/Contacts/Related/Ships.asp*. You can also call your Eldercare Locator at 1-800-677-1116.

- Medicare Health Plan Compare provides the costs and benefits of the Medicare health plans in your area: *www.medicare.gov/MPHCompare/Home.asp*.
- Medigap Compare provides the names and phone numbers of the insurance companies that sell Medigap plans in your state: *www.medicare.gov/mgcompare/home.asp*.

— Medicare Preventive Services —

Preventive health service on your body is like preventive maintenance on your car. Prevention helps them both run better and last longer!

Medicare now provides savvy coverage for many preventive and diagnostic services to help you stay healthy. They include

- Tests for breast cancer, cervical cancer, vaginal cancer and colorectal cancer,
- Bone-mass measurements,
- Diabetes monitoring and diabetes self-management,
- Flu, pneumonia and hepatitis B shots, and
- Prostate cancer screening tests.

Preventive Services

Medicare has made it easier for its beneficiaries to get more diagnostic and preventive care by extending coverage to the following medical treatments and devices:

- Annual dilated-eye exams to detect glaucoma, a leading cause of blindness. These are now covered by Medicare for people at high risk of the disease, including those with diabetes or a family history of glaucoma.
- Medical nutrition therapy, which helps control certain diseases through improved diet. Medicare now covers the services of professional nutritionists for beneficiaries with diabetes or kidney disease.

- Continuous positive airway pressure devices, which are nose masks used to help control sleep apnea, a condition that causes some people to stop breathing for brief periods during sleep.
- Ambulatory blood-pressure monitoring, which involves wearing a cuff that automatically records blood pressure over a 24-hour period. Medicare also covers this system specifically for patients with *white coat hypertension,* a term meaning that just going to the doctor's office is enough to raise their blood pressure, thereby affecting diagnosis.
- Regular foot care for diabetes patients with peripheral neuropathy, a nerve condition that lessens their ability to feel pain, thus increasing the risk of disease and infection that can lead to amputation. Medicare covers two foot exams per year.

For more preventive-care information, call Medicare at 1-800-633-4227 or visit *www.medicare.gov.*

—Hospice Care and Medicare—

Hospice care is a method of caring for the terminally ill that helps provide comfort and support to patients and their families when an illness no longer responds to cure-oriented treatments. Hospice care neither prolongs life nor hastens death. The goal of hospice care is to improve the quality of a patient's last days by offering comfort and dignity. It is provided in the home or a hospice facility, nursing home or hospital. Medical, social, spiritual and counseling services can all be part of hospice care, depending on individual and family needs.

 SAVVY NOTE: Hospice care addresses all symptoms of a disease, with a special emphasis on controlling a patient's pain and discomfort.

Medicare Coverage

Medicare covers hospice care under the Part A, or hospital insurance, portion of the program. You are eligible for Medicare hospice benefits if you are

- Eligible for Medicare Part A.
- Certified as terminally ill (having six months or less to live based on medical knowledge about the normal course of a specific illness) by a doctor and hospice medical director.
- Receiving care from a Medicare-approved hospice program (either through a public agency or private company).

Although a Medicare-approved hospice program includes physicians among the team of trained staff providing care, you may choose to continue under your regular doctor's care. Hospice services are available on an as-needed basis, any time of the day or week.

 SAVVY NOTE: Medicare coverage of hospice care is limited by time periods. You may elect to receive hospice care for up to two periods of 90 days each, followed by an unlimited number of 60-day periods. A physician must certify that you are terminally ill at the beginning of each care period for you to continue receiving care.

Hospice Services Covered Under Medicare

- Physician and nursing care
- Medical supplies and equipment
- Drugs for symptom control and pain relief
- Short-term hospital care, including respite care
- Home health aide and homemaker services
- Physical, occupational and speech therapy
- Medical social services
- Counseling services for patient and family or other caregivers

SAVVY TIP: "Respite" refers to short-term, temporary care provided to people with special needs so that their families can take a break from the daily routine of caregiving. Respite care can be provided in your home, a hospice facility, a nursing home or a hospital. A nice option!

Beneficiary Payments

Medicare pays the hospice directly for care. You are responsible for

- A maximum of $5 for each prescription drug or similar pain-relief and symptom-control product received while not in a hospital or nursing home.
- Five percent of the Medicare payment amount for inpatient respite care. The dollar amount of this copayment will vary depending on the cost of hospice care where you live. The total amount you pay for inpatient respite care during a hospice benefit period cannot exceed the Medicare Part A deductible.

SAVVY RESOURCES

- Medicare puts out the booklet "Medicare Hospice Benefits," which explains the hospice program and its benefits, eligibility requirements and how to find a hospice program. The publication includes telephone numbers for the hospice agency in every state. The book is available in English and Spanish. You can view the book online at *www.medicare.gov/publications/pubs/pdf/hosplg.pdf* or call 1-800-MEDICARE (1-800-633-4227) for your copy.
- Hospice Association of America (HAA): A number of consumer publications are available from this organization. You can order these publications by calling 1-202-546-4759 or visit their Web site at *www.hospice-america.org/consumer.html.*
- Hospice Education Institute: an independent, not-for-profit organization providing members of the public and health-care professionals with information and education about the many facets of caring for the dying and the bereaved. Call 1-800-331-1620 or *www.hospiceworld.org.*

—Home Health Care—

When learning about home health care for yourself or a loved one, remember to ask! Ask for help. Ask for advice. Ask your doctor. Ask another doctor. Ask other family and friends. And don't give up until you have the answers you need.

That said, maybe the first question to ask is: What kinds of services are needed? Home-care providers deliver a wide range of services, including professional nursing and physical, occupational, respiratory and speech therapies. Believe it or not, there are even doctors who still make house calls. There also are homemakers who do light chores such as laundry, general housekeeping and more.

Questions to Ask

When looking at a home-care provider in any of these fields, here are some savvy questions to ask:

- How long have they been in the community? Also, will they provide references from current and past patients or family members? If they don't, drop them. If they do, check them!
- Are they accredited with their respective professional organizations?
- What training does the company provide its employees? What are the years of experience and the training for the specific people who you will be working with?
- Will the company provide a detailed, written statement of the patient's rights and responsibilities, as well as those of the extended family who will be co-operating in the care?
- What are the financial costs and will the company put that in writing?
- What kind of emergency assistance is available for nights and weekends?
- Is the home-health-care provider Medicare certified? That means they have met basic standards set by Uncle Sam.

Medicare Coverage

Medicare Part A pays 100 percent of the cost of your covered home health care provided by a Medicare-approved agency—and there is no limit on the number of visits to your home for which Medicare will pay. To get Medicare home health care

- Your doctor must decide that you need medical care in your home, and make a plan for your care at home;
- You must need at least one of the following: intermittent (and not full-time) skilled-nursing care, physical therapy or speech language pathology services; and
- You must be homebound, or normally unable to leave home unassisted. To be homebound means that leaving home takes considerable and taxing effort. A person may leave home for medical treatment or short, infrequent absences for nonmedical reasons, such as a trip to the barber or to attend religious services.

 SAVVY NOTE: If durable medical equipment is required, such as a special bed or wheelchair, Medicare Part B will pay 80 percent.

Community Support

Don't forget to call upon friends, family and community resources for help and support. Does a church in your community provide volunteers who will visit with homebound disabled and provide companionship, emotional support and maybe even a bit of help with errands? What about Meals on Wheels or other programs available to homebound seniors? It might take some time to arrange, but this could be an important tool for support and recovery.

SAVVY RESOURCES

- Area Agency on Aging: For information on community support programs for homebound seniors, call the Eldercare Locator at 1-800-677-1116.

- Medicare: Their Home Health Compare Web page provides detailed information about home health care and Medicare-certified home health agencies. Call 1-800-633-4227 or visit *www.medicare.gov.*
- National Association for Home Care: See their consumer information at *www.nahc.org.*

—Health-Insurance Help—

Do you know about SHIP? It's a savvy national program that offers free one-on-one counseling and assistance to people with Medicare and their families.

With so much information out there about Medicare, Medicaid and Medigap, it can be mighty difficult to figure out what to do. SHIP (State Health Insurance Program) can provide seniors with a smooth-sailing solution.

Through grants directed to states, SHIPs provide free counseling and assistance via telephone and face-to-face interactive sessions, public education presentations and programs and media activities. Currently, there are SHIPs in all 50 states plus Washington, D.C., Puerto Rico and the Virgin Islands.

SHIP Services

Specially trained SHIP counselors offer information, counseling and assistance to people with Medicare on Medicare, Medicaid, Medigap, long-term-care insurance and preventive care. These counselors have direct access to state and federal Medicare information. They can

- Inform you on the new Medicare reform changes and prescription drug benefit and help you review and understand your options.
- Explain your Original Medicare benefits by detailing which services are covered under Parts A and B, and help you understand your Medicare Summary notice.

- Help you make informed choices about Medicare coverage options, including the Medicare + Choice options.
- Provide assistance and information on Medicare claims and billing problems as well as Medicare appeals and assist with appeals paperwork.
- Help you select a Medigap insurance policy by explaining the benefits offered under each plan and by providing you with a list of companies that sell Medigap plans.
- Inform you about eligibility for prescription-drug programs and programs that pay Medicare deductibles, copayments and Part B premiums.
- Provide information on public-benefit programs for those with limited income and assets.
- Inform you about Medicare fraud and abuse.

Volunteer SHIP Mates

SHIPs for the most part are made up of a network of volunteers supported by local sponsoring organizations. Paid staff manage these local programs and serve as SHIP counselors. Under the direction and support of state program directors and trainers, SHIP counselors receive extensive training and continuous ongoing information updates about Medicare and other health-insurance topics.

Currently the SHIP network nationwide includes close to 1,100 sponsoring organizations supporting over 12,000 counselors and staff. Last year alone, the SHIPs served over 3 million Medicare beneficiaries, with about 2.5 million of those served through one-on-one, in-person and over-the-telephone counseling sessions and approximately 500,000 served through SHIP presentations and public-education programs. In addition, SHIPs help beneficiaries through approximately 20,000 outreach events and media activities conducted annually.

 SAVVY NOTE: Contact SHIP if you are interested in becoming a volunteer.

SHIP Contact Information

State and local SHIP organizations and phone numbers can be found at *www.medicare.gov/Contacts/Related/Ships.asp* or by contacting Medicare at 1-800-633-4227. You can also call your Eldercare Locator at 1-800-677-1116.

 SAVVY NOTE: Some states will have a different name for their SHIP, but they usually cover the same services. Always ask for your state health-insurance counseling program!

—Medicaid and Nursing-Home Care—

If you're trying to figure out how to pay for your or your loved one's nursing-home care, the following information might be just what the doctor ordered!

Nursing-home care is very expensive, averaging over $50,000 a year in 2004, depending on where you live and what you choose. That's why many nursing-home residents pay the full cost when they are admitted, but they deplete their savings and other assets and qualify for Medicaid.

 SAVVY NOTE: Almost 70 percent of nursing-home residents receive help from Medicaid.

Does Medicare Pay?

No. Medicare does not pay for long-term care. It covers only short periods of skilled-nursing-home care after a hospital stay.

What Does Medicaid Pay For?

- Medicaid will pay the part of your nursing-home costs that your own income doesn't cover. In most states, a nursing-home patient cannot keep more than $30 to $50 a month for personal needs.

- Medicaid will cover all your nursing-home care as well as some basic needs, such as toiletries and over-the-counter medications. It will not pay for clothing.
- Medicaid will pay for prescription drugs and some other services not paid for by Medicare.

 SAVVY NOTE: The Medicaid program provides medical assistance for certain individuals and families with low incomes and resources. Medicaid is funded and regulated by both the federal and state governments. This means that Medicaid rules differ from state to state. It's wise to learn your state's specific requirements.

Medicaid Eligibility

To be eligible to receive Medicaid for nursing-home care, an individual must:

- Have savings and other assets below your state's required amount (usually between $1,000 and $4,000). Some assets may not counted, such as your house, car or a burial fund.
- Meet the income requirements set by the state.
- Undergo a screening to make sure you meet the state's medical and functional criteria for nursing-home care.

 SAVVY NOTE: To use Medicaid, you must be in a nursing home that accepts Medicaid. Most do!

Does the Spouse of a Nursing-Home Patient Get Wiped Out?

No. The spouse's financial resources will be protected to the maximum extent allowed by the law. If the nursing-home patient is receiving Medicaid, it is important to know your state's policies on spousal protection. Here's the general 2004 breakdown for the spouse:

- In most states, the spouse can keep a monthly income of up to the federal maximum of $2,319.

- The spouse can keep half of the couple's combined assets, up to a maximum of $92,760.

- The spouse can keep the couple's home and surrounding property, if they live there. If they move, the house and property becomes an asset that will affect Medicaid.

SAVVY NOTE: If the spouse's monthly income is under $2,319, the Spousal Impoverishment program will allow the nursing-home patient to use a portion of their monthly income to raise the spouse's income, up to the federal maximum of $2,319 per month.

Transferring Your Assets

If you're looking to transfer your assets to your heirs, hoping to fall back on Medicaid if you should need long-term care, *beware*! The government is allowed to examine the last three years of your financial transactions at the time you apply for Medicaid. If a transfer was made to defraud Uncle Sam and make it seem you have no assets, you could be subject to fines and even jail.

Good to Know

Did you know that nursing homes

- Cannot make you agree to pay privately for care for a period of time before you apply for Medicaid or make a "donation" in order to be admitted?

- Cannot require a third party (for example, a son or daughter) to guarantee to pay for your care?

- Cannot discharge you because you become eligible for Medicaid?

- Cannot make you pay privately for any services or products that are covered by your state's Medicaid program?

More Information

Contact your state or county Department of Human Services office, or county Medicaid office. They can provide information about Medicaid eligibility in your state.

Call the Eldercare Locator at 1-800-677-1116 for the phone numbers of these offices in your community.

SAVVY RESOURCES

- American Public Human Services Association: links to each state's Medicaid information. Log on to *www.aphsa.org*.
- National Council on the Aging Benefits Check-Up: a free service to help older Americans identify state and federal assistance. Visit *www .benefitscheckup.org*.
- Center for Medicaid and Medicare Services (CMS). Provides information relating to Medicaid- and Medicare-certified nursing homes throughout the United States. Call 1-800-633-4227 or visit *www.cms.gov*.

—Medicare Fraud—

Have you ever felt concerned, surprised or not quite right about a doctor's bill you received? If so, call 1-800-447-8477 and join the fight against Medicare fraud. Last year the Medicare program lost billions due to fraud and abuse.

Who pays for the money lost due to Medicare fraud? YOU DO, by paying higher Medicare premiums.

Fraud and abuse affect everyone—those with Medicare and Medicaid as well as those with private insurance. They contribute to the rising cost of health care and, in some instances, diminish the quality of care provided.

 SAVVY NOTE: Most Medicare payment errors are simple mistakes and are not the result of physicians, providers or suppliers trying to take advantage of the Medicare system.

Fraud Defense

You can help spot questionable Medicare charges by taking three savvy steps.

Your first step is to check each Medicare statement you receive and answer these three questions about the charges:

- Did you receive the service or product for which Medicare is being billed?
- Did your doctor order the service or product for you?
- To the best of your knowledge, is the service or product relevant to your diagnosis or treatment? (If you have a question about a procedure or test, ask your doctor to explain the need for it.)

Your second step is to get a second opinion if you spot something questionable. Call your provider first. The charge could be a simple billing error. If you can't easily resolve your questions with the provider, you should report the questionable charges to your Medicare carrier for clarification. This number can be found at the top of your Medicare statement.

Your final step is to report a questionable charge to the Medicare Fraud Hotline at 1-800-447-8477.

Savvy Tips

- Treat your Medicare card like a credit card. Never give out your Medicare number over the phone unless you initiated the call. If your card is lost or stolen, report it immediately.
- Don't accept free medical equipment or services in exchange for your Medicare number. Nothing is ever free. Unscrupulous providers could bill Medicare for services or equipment you may never have received.
- Stay informed. Know which services or equipment you are supposed to receive so you can avoid getting something you don't need.
- Be alert for those who claim to "know how to bill Medicare" to get an uncovered item or service paid for: It's a scam. Report it immediately.

Be on the Lookout

Federal authorities have identified the most typical fraudulent practices you should be watching for. Here are some examples:

- Charging more than once for the same service (double billing)
- Charging for services never performed or medical equipment or supplies that were never ordered
- Performing inappropriate or unnecessary services
- Offering free services or medical equipment in exchange for your Medicare, Medicaid or private insurance number
- Providing lower-cost or used equipment while billing Medicare for higher-cost or new equipment
- A supplier completing a Certificate of Medical Necessity form for a physician

SAVVY RESOURCES

- Medicare: The official government Medicare Web site has additional information about antifraud activities. Visit *www.medicare.gov/ FraudAbuse/Overview.asp.*
- Department of Health and Human Services: They have fraud alerts and advisory bulletins about the ongoing efforts to stop Medicare fraud. Visit *www.dhhs.gov.*

—Cost-Cutting Tips on Prescription Drugs—

Every year, many seniors across the United States become ill and die because they can't afford to purchase the prescription medication(s) they need. This is a tragedy!

The new Medicare drug benefit that will begin in 2006 will help some seniors, depending on their income level and how much they spend on prescription drugs per year, but savings for most will be minimal. So, with help from the Medicare Rights Center, *The Savvy Senior* has developed a comprehensive list of available prescription-drug discount options.* You should never be forced to stop taking medicines because you can't afford them. With some discount assistance, maybe now you won't have to.

 SAVVY FACT: The typical American over the age of 65 takes an average of six prescription drugs.

- **Ask Your Doctor:** Many doctors have extra supplies of various medications in their offices and are willing to help out their patients in need.
- **Go Generic:** Purchase generic drugs if your doctor agrees a generic will work. Prices for generic drugs are often cheaper in the United States than abroad and are cheapest of all at bargain chains like Costco (see Internet-Based Discount Programs, page 179, for contact information).
- **Contact the Drug Maker:** Many pharmaceutical companies give away free prescription drugs to consumers who can't afford them. Most programs are limited to low-income households, but a handful of the more expensive drugs are available to people with incomes of $30,000 a year or more.

 SAVVY NOTE: Each company has its own distinct application process. For a free directory of patient-assistance programs, call the Pharmaceutical Research and Manufacturers of America at 1-800-762-4636 or visit online at *www.phrma.org*.

NATIONAL PRESCRIPTION-DRUG ASSISTANCE PROGRAMS

Eligibility for these programs is based on age, income or medical condition.

- **AIDS Drug Assistance Program (ADAP):** Must be low-income, uninsured or underinsured, with HIV/AIDS. State-sponsored program provides

---

* The discount options listed in this chapter are subject to change. See *www.medicarerights.org* for any new or updated discount information.

prescriptions for HIV/AIDS treatment. Visit *www.atdn.org/access/states/index.html*.

- **Medicaid:** Full Medicaid or Medicaid Excess Income Program "spend-down." Income limits vary by state. Call your state Medicaid office for more information.

- **National Organization for Rare Disorders (NORD):** NORD's Medication Assistance Programs help people obtain prescriptions they could not otherwise afford or that are not yet on the market. Over 1,100 rare diseases are listed on NORD's Web site, including AIDS, Alzheimer's disease, multiple sclerosis and Parkinson's disease: Call 1-203-746-6518 or visit *www.rarediseases.org*.

- **Pharmaceutical Company Patient Assistance Programs (PhRMA):** For low-income patients with no other prescription coverage. Free or heavily discounted prescriptions for limited duration (often 90 days). Prescription is sent directly from drug company to physician. To find out which company makes each prescription and to apply, ask your doctor for assistance. The Medicine Program (1-573-996-7300) will help you with the application process for a fee of $5 per prescription. Call 1-202-835-3400 or visit *www.rxassist.org* or *www.needymeds.com* for a directory of programs.

- **TRICARE:** Offers low-cost prescriptions to military retirees who have served at least 20 years. Must be registered with Defense Enrollment Eligibility Reporting System (DEERS). No enrollment fees. Call 1-877-363-6337.

- **VA Health Benefits Service Center:** Offers free prescriptions for low-income veterans, with a $7 fee per prescription for all other veterans. Veteran must have been honorably discharged from the military. Must enroll with VA and be seen by VA doctor. Call 1-877-222-8387.

STATE PRESCRIPTION-DRUG
ASSISTANCE PROGRAMS

Special programs for low-income people with Medicare are offered by 25 states, including

California

Prescription Drug Discount Program for Medicare Recipients: 1-800-434-0222

Connecticut

Connecticut Pharmaceutical Assistance Contract to the Elderly and Disabled Program (ConnPACE): 1-800-423-5026 (Connecticut residents only) or 1-860-832-9265, *www.connpace.com*

Delaware

Nemours Health Clinic Pharmacy Assistance: 1-800-292-9538, *www.nemours.org/no/nhc/svcs/pharmceutical.html*

Florida

Silver Saver Program: 1-888-419-3456 or call local Medicaid office, *www .floridahealthstat.com/rxstat.shtml*

Illinois

Illinois Pharmaceutical Assistance Program (PAP): 1-800-624-2459 or 1-800-544-5304 (TDD), *www.revenue.state.il.us/CircuitBreaker*

Indiana

HoosierRx: 1-866-267-4679, *www.state.in.us/fssa/rxprogram/rxhome.htm*

Iowa

Iowa Priority Prescription Savings Program: 1-866-282-5817, *www.iowapriority.org*

Maine

Maine Low Cost Drugs for the Elderly and Disabled (DEL) Program: 1-888-600-2466, 1-866-796-2463, 1-207-622-3210 (TTY), *www.state.me.us/dhs/beas/ medbook.htm*

Healthy Maine Prescriptions: 1-866-796-2463, *www.state.me.us/bms/ hmpwebsite/howtoapply.html*

Maryland

Maryland Pharmacy Assistance Program (MPAP): 1-800-492-1974 or 1-410-767-5394, *www.dhmh.state.md.us/mma/mpap*

Maryland Short-Term Prescription Drug Subsidy Plan: 1-800-972-4612, *www.carefirst.com*

Maryland Medbank Program: 1-410-821-9262, *www.medbankmd.org*

Massachusetts

Prescription Advantage: 1-800-243-4636, *www.800ageinfo.com*

Michigan

Elder Prescription Insurance Coverage (EPIC): 1-866-747-5844, *www.miepic.com*

Minnesota

Minnesota Prescription Drug Program: 1-800-333-2433, *www.dhs.state.mn.us/hlthcare/asstprog/prescription_drugs.htm*

Missouri

Missouri SenioRx: 1-866-556-9316, *www.missouriseniorx.com*

Nevada

Senior Rx (through Fidelity Security Life Insurance): 1-800-262-7726, *www.nevadaseniorrx.com*

New Hampshire

New Hampshire Senior Prescription Drug Discount Program: 1-888-580-8902, *www.dhhs.state.nh.us/DHHS/DEAS/B2.htm*

New Jersey

Pharmaceutical Assistance to the Aged and Disabled Program (PAAD): 1-800-792-9745, *www.state.nj.us/health/seniorbenefits/paadapp.htm*

Senior Gold Prescription Discount Program: 1-800-792-9745, *www.state.nj.us/health/seniorbenefits/seniorgolddiscount.htm*

New York

Elderly Pharmaceutical Insurance Coverage (EPIC): 1-800-332-3742, *www.health.state.ny.us/nysdoh/epic/faq.htm*

North Carolina

Senior Care: 1-800-226-1388, *www.ncseniorcare.com*

Senior PharmAssist: 1-919-688-4772, *www.seniorpharmassist.org*

Pennsylvania

Pharmaceutical Assistance Contract for the Elderly (PACE): 1-800-225-7223,

1-717-787-7313, *www.aging.state.pa.us/aging/cwp/view.asp?a=293&Q=173876*

Pharmaceutical Assistance Contract for the Elderly Needs Enhancement Tier

(PACENET): 1-800-225-7223, 1-717-787-7313,

www.aging.state.pa.us/aging/cwp/view.asp?a=293&Q=173876

Rhode Island

Rhode Island Pharmaceutical Assistance for the Elderly: 1-401-222-3330

South Carolina

SILVERx CARD: 1-877-239-5277, *www.silverxcard.com*

Commun-I-Care: 1-800-763-0059, 1-803-933-9183, *www.commun-i-care.org*

Vermont

Vermont Health Access Plan-Pharmacy: 1-800-250-8427,

www.dsw.state.vt.us/districts/ovha/ovha10.htm

VSCRIPT: 1-800-250-8427, *www.dsw.state.vt.us/districts/ovha/ovha10.htm*

VSCRIPT- EXPANDED: 1-800-250-8427,

www.dsw.state.vt.us/districts/ovha/ovha10.html

West Virginia

Golden Mountaineer Discount Card: 1-877-987-3646, 1-304-558-3317,

www.state.wv.us/seniorservices

Wisconsin

SeniorCare—Levels 1, 2 and 3: 1-800-657-2038, *www.dhfs.state.wi.us/seniorcare*

Wyoming

Prescription Drug Assistance Program: 1-800-442-2766, 1-307-777-7986

PRESCRIPTION-DRUG DISCOUNT CARDS

Members may use discount cards at participating pharmacies to get non-Medicare-covered items. Some programs also offer discounts of up to 60 percent on vision, dental and hearing services.

- **AARP Member Choice Program:** Discounts for AARP members. AARP membership plus $15/person annual fee. 1-800-439-4457, *www.rpspharmacy.com*
- **Costco:** Discounts for Costco members. Online pharmacy also available. Discount depends on prescriptions. Basic membership: $45/family annual fee or Executive plan: $100/family annual fee. 1-800-955-2292, *www.costco.com*
- **GSK Orange Card:** Must have no other prescription coverage. Discounts on GlaxoSmithKline prescriptions only. No fee. Up to 30 percent discount depending on prescriptions. Annual income must be less than $26,000 (single) or $35,000 (couple). 1-888-672-6436
- **LillyAnswers Card:** Must have no other prescription coverage. Discounts on Eli Lilly prescriptions only. No fee. Annual income must be less than $18,000 (single) or $24,000 (couple). Cost: $12/prescription up to a 30-day supply. 1-877-795-4559, *www.lillyanswers.com*
- **Mature Rx:** Up to 65 percent discount depending on prescriptions. No fee. 1-800-511-1314, *www.maturerx.com*
- **Merck Medco:** Discounts on prescriptions. Annual fee: $25/person or $40/family. 1-877-733-6765, *www.yourplan.com*
- **Novartis CareCard:** Discounts on Novartis only. No fee. Annual income must be less than $26,000 (single) or $35,000 (couple). 1-866-974-2273, *www.novartis.com*
- **Peoples Prescription Plan:** Discounts on prescriptions, eyeglasses and hearing aids. Dental plan also available. Monthly fee: $7.95/family. Up to 50 percent discount depending on prescription. 1-800-566-0003, *www.peoplesrxcard.com*
- **Pfizer Share Card:** Discounts on Pfizer only. No fee. Annual income must be less than $18,000 (single) or $24,000 (couple). Cost: $15/prescription up to a 30-day supply. 1-800-717-6005, *www.pfizerforliving.com*
- **Prescription Benefits, Inc.:** Discounts on prescriptions. Annual fee: $48/person or $60/family. Up to 90 percent discount depending on prescription. 1-800-377-1614, *www.rxbenefits.com*
- **RxDrugCard:** Discounts on prescriptions. Annual fee: $45.95/person or $49.95/family. Discount depends on prescription. Deeper discounts at

Kmart pharmacies for 90-day supply. 1-888-216-2461, *www.rxdrugcard .com*

- **Rx Power:** Discount plans include prescriptions, vitamins/nutrition, dental, vision, hearing. Basic plan annual fee: $41/family. Comprehensive plan annual fee: $65/family. Discounts range from 15 to 60 percent depending on prescription. 1-877-797-6937, *www.rxpower.com*

- **Together Rx:** Must have no other prescription coverage. Annual income must be less than $28,000 (single) or $38,000 (couple). No fee. Discounts range from 15 to 40 percent depending on prescription. 1-800-865-7211, *www.togetherrx.com*

- **United States Pharmaceutical Group, Inc.:** Discount plans include prescriptions, dental, vision, hearing, diabetic and respiratory supplies and chiropractic care. Mail-order service also available. No fee. Up to 21 percent discount depending on prescription. 1-800-977-9655, *www.uspgi.com*

MAIL-ORDER DISCOUNT PHARMACIES

These pharmacies offer discounts of up to 60 percent when people order prescriptions by mail. Some also have discounted prices on over-the-counter medications and diabetic supplies. Most do not charge membership fees, but there may be shipping and handling costs. Because advertised savings are often the result of substituting generic for brand-name drugs, call for the price of your prescriptions.

- **Advanta 65 Health Services:** Specializes in diabetic and respiratory supplies. No fee. Discount depends on item. 1-800-682-8283, *www.advantagerx.com*

- **APP Pharmacy:** Specializes in long-term and chronic medications. No fee. Discount depends on prescription. 1-800-227-1195, *www.apppharmacy.com*

- **DrugPlace.com:** Discounts on generic prescriptions only. Shipping and handling fees apply. Discount depends on manufacturers' current prices. 1-800-881-6325, *www.drugplace.com*

- **Drugspot.com:** Discounts on prescriptions. $5.95 monthly fee. Discount: 15 percent off brand-name, 50 percent off generic prescriptions. 1-800-707-2279, *www.drugspot.com*

- **Express Script:** Discounts on prescriptions, dental, hearing and eye care. Discount depends on quantity and manufacturer's current price. 1-800-854-4469, *www.express-script.com*

- **Liberty Health Supply:** Specializes in diabetic and respiratory supplies. Discount depends on item. 1-800-398-6514 (diabetes), 1-800-894-3028 (respiratory), *www.libertymedical.com*

- **Mature Rx:** Discounts on prescriptions. No fee. 1-800-511-1314, *www.maturerx.com*

- **Postal Prescription Services:** Discounts on 30-, 60- and 90-day supplies. Annual fee: $10. Discount: 10 percent. 1-800-552-6694, *www.ppsrx.com/ppsrx/home.do*

- **Rx Power:** Discounts on prescriptions. Other discount plans include vitamins/nutrition, dental, vision, hearing. Basic plan annual fee: $41/family. Comprehensive plan annual fee: $65/family. Shipping and handling fees apply. Discounts range from 15 to 60 percent. 1-877-797-6937, *www.rxpower.com*

- **Rx Universe/PSG:** Limit 3-month supply. Annual fee: $20/person or $35/family. Shipping and handling fees apply. Discounts range from 12 to 15 percent. 1-800-794-6490, *www.rxuniverse.com*

- **United States Pharmaceutical Group, Inc.:** Discount plans include prescriptions, dental, vision, hearing, diabetic and respiratory supplies and chiropractic care. No fee. Up to 21 percent discount depending on prescription. 1-800-977-9655, *www.uspgi.com*

INTERNET-BASED DISCOUNT PROGRAMS

For a list comparing current drug prices offered by online pharmacies, visit *www.destinationrx.com*. Also, to find out how to buy prescriptions online safely and securely, call 1-888-463-6332 or go to *www.fda.gov*.

- **www.pharmacychecker.com:** Compare prescription prices across pharmacies for 1,000+ medications. You'll also see shipping and other fees so you can compare total costs, along with ratings of each online pharmacy.

- **www.canadadrugs.com:** More than 2,300 prescriptions available from Manitoba Pharmacy Association. Discount depends on prescription. 1-800-226-3784, *pharmacists@canadadrugs.com*
- **www.canadapharmacy.com:** Discount depends on prescription. Shipping and handling fee of $10/order. 1-800-891-0844, *customerservice@ canadapharmacy.com*
- **www.canadameds.com:** Discounts on prescriptions, diabetic supplies, vitamins/nutrition and home health-care items. Shipping and handling fee of $13/prescription package. Discounts range from 30 to 70 percent. 1-877-542-3330, *pharmacists@canadameds.com*
- **www.canadarx.net:** Specializes in chronic and acute prescriptions and HIV/AIDS treatment. Limit 3-month supply. You can order mail-order prescriptions from the United States or make appointments to purchase prescription drugs at participating Canadian pharmacies. Shipping and handling fee: $9.99/item. Discount depends on prescription. Prices are in Canadian dollars.
- **www.thecanadiandrugstore.com:** Specializes in chronic-care prescriptions. Shipping and handling fee of $14/package. Discount depends on prescription. 1-888-372-2252
- **www.medicationscanada.com:** 1-866-481-5817, *pharmacist@ medicationscanada.com*
- **www.canadianmedservice.com:** 1-866-887-0688, *info@canadianmedservice .com*
- **www.adv-care.com:** Discounts on more than 20,000 prescription and health and beauty items. *pharmacist@adv-care.com*
- **www.costco.com:** Online pharmacy enables you to order online for home delivery or pickup at local Costco warehouse. Basic membership: $45/family. Executive plan: $100/family. Free standard delivery. Discounts range from 20 to 50 percent. 1-800-955-2292
- **www.drugstore.com:** Discount depends on prescription. Shipping and handling fees range from $1.49 to $16.95. 1-800-378-4786

- **www.eckerd.com:** Discounts on prescriptions. Online pharmacy enables you to order online for home delivery or pickup at local Eckerd pharmacy. Free standard delivery. Discount depends on prescription. 1-800-325-3737
- **www.familymeds.com:** Discount depends on prescriptions. Free standard delivery. 1-888-787-2800
- **www.homemed.com:** Discounts on prescriptions. Shipping and handling fees range from $1.95 to $35. 1-888-726-4496, *customer.service@homemed.com*
- **www.rxnorth.com:** Discounts on prescriptions and diabetic supplies. Shipping and handling fee of $15/order. 1-888-773-2698

SAVVY RESOURCES

- Benefits Check-Up: The National Council on Aging offers its free BenefitsCheck-UpRx. This online service provides a confidential, personalized report of public and private programs that can help you save money on some or all of your prescription drugs. They will check your potential eligibility for over 260 programs covering more than 1,450 prescription drugs. Visit *www.benefitscheckup.org*.
- Medicare Prescription-Drug Assistance Program: Provides information on public and private programs that offer discounted or free medication, as well as Medicare health plans that include prescription coverage. Visit *www.Medicare.gov*.

SOCIAL SECURITY

OVER 50 PERCENT OF THE MANY QUESTIONS THE SAVVY SENIOR COLUMN
receives are about Social Security. Whether it's deciding at what age to start drawing
your Social Security retirement benefits or how to apply for Social Security disability,
this section simplifies the bare basics of Social Security. Included are chapters on retirement benefits, survivors benefits, taxation, how work affects your Social Security,
the appeals process and the Social Security age increases that are currently in effect.

Other topics include SSI, how divorced widows can tap into their deceased ex-
husbands' Social Security benefits and the controversy still surrounding the group of
seniors called *notch babies.*

—Social Security Retirement Basics—

Does Social Security leave you feeling a little insecure?

Since President Roosevelt signed the Social Security Act into law in 1935, Social Security has evolved from a modest Depression-era experiment into a huge financial protection program that covers 95 percent of the U.S. workforce. More than 45 million people (almost one out of every six Americans) collect Social Security benefits each month.

Although Social Security was never intended to be a retiree's only source of income, it has become the largest single source, providing 90 percent or more of all income to one-third of its beneficiaries, and over 20 percent of seniors 65 and older are living solely on their Social Security checks.

 SAVVY NOTE: The poverty rate among senior citizens in the United States is almost 10 percent. Without Social Security retirement benefits, the senior citizen poverty rate would be over 40 percent.

A Simple Concept That Gets Confusing

Social Security is based on a simple concept. When you work, you pay taxes into the Social Security system, and when you retire or become disabled, you, your spouse and your dependent children receive monthly benefits that are based on your earnings. And your survivors collect benefits when you die.

 SAVVY NOTE: Social Security benefits are not intended to meet all of your financial needs. When you retire, you'll need other income, such as savings or a pension. Think of Social Security as a foundation upon which to build a financial future.

Social Security "Credits"

To receive Social Security retirement benefits, you must work and pay taxes into Social Security in order to be eligible. (Of course, some people get benefits as dependents or survivors on other persons' Social Security records.)

As you work and pay taxes, you earn Social Security *credits*. In the year 2004, you earn one credit for each $900 in earnings you have—up to a maximum of four credits per year (the amount of money needed to earn one credit goes up every year).

Most people need 40 credits (10 years of work) to qualify for benefits. Younger people need fewer credits to be eligible for disability benefits or for family members to be eligible for survivors benefits if the worker dies.

 SAVVY NOTE: During your working lifetime, you probably will earn more credits than you need to be eligible for Social Security; these extra credits, however, do not increase your eventual Social Security benefit. But the income you earn may increase your benefit.

How Much Will I Get from Social Security?

- Earnings History: Retirement benefits are based primarily on your averaged earnings during a 35-year career. So, the more money you made (and paid into Social Security), the more your retirement benefits will be (up to an inflation-adjusted cap).
- Age: Full retirement benefits are paid at age 65 and 4 months in 2004 (see entire Social Security Age Scale on page 190); workers who retire at age 62 get a reduced benefit based on the likelihood of their collecting benefits over a longer period of time (see Social Security Benefits: Now or Later?, page 191). Workers who postpone retirement beyond full retirement age up to age 70 get more than the full benefit. Survivors and disability benefits also are determined by a worker's average earnings (see Survivors Benefits, page 194, and Social Security Disability, page 203).

Who Else Gets Benefits?

When you start collecting Social Security retirement or disability benefits, other members of your family also may be eligible for payments. For example, benefits can be paid to

- Your spouse, if he or she is age 62 or older (unless he or she collects a higher Social Security benefit on his or her own record);
- Your spouse at any age, if he or she is caring for your child (the child must be under age 16 or disabled and receiving Social Security benefits); and
- Your children, if they are unmarried and under age 18; under age 19, but in elementary or secondary school as full-time students; or age 18 or older and severely disabled (the disability must have started before age 22).

How Much Can Family Members Get?

Each family member may be eligible for a monthly benefit that is up to 50 percent of your retirement or disability benefit amount. However, there's a limit to the total amount of money that can be paid to a family on your Social Security record.

Attention Homemakers

You may be eligible for a spouse's benefits if you are married! If you make your home and family your career, you and your family have Social Security protection through your spouse's work, and are eligible to receive benefits when he or she retires, becomes disabled or dies.

You also are eligible to receive benefits if you are caring for a child who is under age 16 or disabled and entitled to benefits. If you don't have a child in your care, you must be age 62 or older to get benefits when your spouse becomes disabled or retires.

If you choose to begin receiving retirement benefits before full retirement age, your benefit amount will be permanently reduced. If you wait until you're at full retirement age, you'll get the full benefits, which come to 50 percent of the amount your spouse is entitled to at full retirement age.

You and your spouse will have Medicare hospital insurance at age 65 if he or she will be eligible for monthly benefits, and you both may sign up for medical insurance. You will have Medicare at age 65 even if your spouse is younger than you and still working, provided he or she is at least age 62 and will be eligible for benefits at retirement.

How to File

When you're ready to file for retirement benefits, you may choose one of these easy methods:

- File your application online at *www.socialsecurity.gov*.
- Call 1-800-772-1213 to file by telephone.
- Call the toll-free number to make an appointment to visit a local Social Security office to file for benefits.

SAVVY NOTES: If you're just thinking about filing for retirement benefits, you should talk with a Social Security representative a few months before the year you plan to retire. To file for disability, survivors or SSI benefits, you should apply as soon as you're eligible. You must call or visit a Social Security office to file for these benefits.

For Social Security questions, call 1-800-772-1213, Monday through Friday, between 7 A.M. and 7 P.M., or visit their Web site at *www.socialsecurity.gov*. If you are deaf or hard of hearing, call the TTY number: 1-800-325-0778.

SAVVY RESOURCE

- Social Security offers a free booklet called "Understanding the Benefits," publication no. 05-10024, or you can visit it online at *www.ssa.gov/pubs/10024/html*.

—Social Security Age Hike—

If you haven't paid attention, you may not know that Social Security has hiked up the age at which seniors born after 1937 may receive full retirement benefits.

Changing demographics are the driving force behind the rising age change in the Social Security system. Americans are living longer and healthier lives, which is good news! When the Social Security program was created in 1935, a 65-year-old had an average life expectancy of 12.5 more years. Today it's 17.5 years—and rising. In addition, 77 million baby boomers will begin retiring by 2010, and in about 30 years, there will be nearly twice as many older Americans as there are today. At the same time, the number of workers paying into Social Security per beneficiary will drop from 3.4 to 2.1. These changes will strain the retirement system.

 SAVVY FACTS: In 1950, Americans age 65 and older totaled 13 million. In 2000 that number totaled 35 million, and by the year 2030, it will rise to 71 million.

Social Security Options

Choosing when to get Social Security retirement benefits is up to you. You may retire when you reach full retirement age and get your full retirement benefits. You may retire before reaching full retirement age and get "reduced" benefits. Or, you may choose to work beyond full retirement age. If that's your choice, you have two more options. You can get retirement benefits while working. Or, if you continue working and choose to delay getting retirement benefits until you reach age 70, you'll earn credits that increase your benefit amount. For more information on when to start your retirement benefits, see Social Security Benefits: Now or Later?, page 191.

SOCIAL SECURITY AGE SCALE

If you were born before 1938, you will be eligible for your full Social Security benefits at the age of 65. However, in 2003, the age at which full benefits are payable increased in gradual steps from 65 to 67. Here's the breakdown:

Year of Birth	Full Retirement Age	Surviving Spouse's Full Retirement Age
1937 or earlier	65	65
1938	65 and 2 months	65
1939	65 and 4 months	65
1940	65 and 6 months	65 and 2 months
1941	65 and 8 months	65 and 4 months
1942	65 and 10 months	65 and 6 months
1943	66	65 and 8 months
1944	66	65 and 10 months
1945-54	66	66
1955	66 and 2 months	66
1956	66 and 4 months	66
1957	66 and 6 months	66 and 2 months
1958	66 and 8 months	66 and 4 months
1959	66 and 10 months	66 and 6 months
1960	67	66 and 8 months
1961	67	66 and 10 months
1962 and later	67	67

Reduced Benefits Still Start at Age 62

No matter what your full retirement age is, you may start receiving benefits as early as age 62. However, if you start your benefits early, they are reduced five-ninths of 1 percent for each month before your full retirement age. For example, if your full retirement age is 66 (born between 1943 and 1954) and you sign up for Social Security when you're 65, you will receive around 93 percent of your full benefit. At age 62, you would get around 75 percent.

 SAVVY NOTE: The reduction will be greater (up to 30 percent) in future years as the full retirement age increases.

—Social Security Benefits: Now or Later?—

Figuring out when to start collecting your Social Security retirement benefits is a big decision. Should you start collecting benefits early and take less, or wait for more later—but what if you die?

There's no right answer on this issue, because whatever you decide to do, you're gambling with Uncle Sam. But before you lay down your bet, be sure to visit your local Social Security office to get all the facts. Social Security has formulas that roughly match your life expectancy with the benefits you get. If you live longer than expected, you get more than the government planned to pay you. But if you die too soon, Uncle Sam wins.

When Should I Start Collecting?

- You can begin collecting benefits as early as age 62—before your full retirement age. But if you do, your benefits will be reduced to account for the longer period over which you'll be paid.
- You can begin collecting full benefits at age 65 if you were born before 1938. The "full" retirement age has been ratcheted up for everyone else—up to 67 for those born in 1960 or later.
- You can forgo collecting benefits up until you turn 70 and thus qualify for a "delayed retirement credit." If you do, your eventual monthly benefit will go up by as much as 8 percent for each year beyond your full retirement age that you put off receiving benefits.

Which Choice Is Best?

Although all three options are designed to eventually pay out roughly equal total amounts, 6 in 10 retirees opt for the early benefits.

Benefit Payout Example

Say that you turn 62 in 2004 and will be eligible, based on your lifetime earnings, for a monthly benefit of $804 a month. Wait until your full retirement age (which would be 65 and 10 months) in 2008, and the benefit will be $1,255 a month. Delay the benefits until you're 70, in 2012, and you'll get $1,991 a month.

 SAVVY NOTE: This example is figured using the Social Security Administration's inflated (future) dollars scale, at *www.socialsecurity.gov.*

Other Factors to Consider

- Your Health and Life Expectancy: While you can't outlive your Social Security benefits, taking them can change from a smart move to a not-so-smart move if you live long enough. It's a gamble, but if you expect to live long because of good health and family longevity, you may be wise not to take benefits early.

 SAVVY FACT: If you live to age 65, your average life expectancy today for a man is about 81, and for a woman it is 84.

- Your Spouse's Income Needs: Your spouse's needs could be a big factor if he or she is much younger and likely to collect survivors benefits for many, many years. If your spouse is not in the paid labor force, your Social Security benefits could represent the lion's share of his or her retirement income in the future.
- The Power of Money: Don't forget that the money you already have in retirement accounts could keep growing tax deferred if you were to live instead on Social Security benefits.
- How Long You Want to Keep Working: Work often provides health-care coverage and other benefits that can otherwise cost you plenty. If you want to keep working, collecting benefits before you reach full retirement age probably doesn't make sense, especially if you have considerable earnings. That's

because your Social Security benefits are reduced if you earn above a certain ceiling, which is adjusted each year.

Sooner or Later

The Social Security formulas for early, full and delayed benefits are designed to be a wash over your lifetime. But that's based on average life expectancy. About 60 percent choose to take benefits early because the break-even point is after age 80. If you don't survive to 80, then it would be a mistake not to take early benefits.

Experts also agree there's almost never any reason to wait to take benefits until you turn 70, unless you have a much younger spouse who will need your benefits to meet living expenses after you die.

This information was obtained in part from AARP and the Social Security Administration.

 SAVVY TIP: Social Security offers a "Retirement Planner" on their Web site that includes online calculators to help you estimate how much you will get at different ages based on your current and future earnings. Visit *www.socialsecurity.gov/r&m1.htm*.

Direct-Deposit Your Benefits

If you're not already doing so, direct deposit is a simple, safe and secure way to receive federal payments like Social Security and Veterans benefits. Statistics show that recipients are 20 times more likely to have a problem with a paper check than with a direct-deposit transaction.

To sign up for direct deposit, you may complete a simple form available from a local financial institution, contact the federal agency that issues benefit payments or call Social Security at 1-800-772-1213. If you do not have an account at a financial institution, you may sign up for the Treasury Department's electronic transfer account (ETA).

For more information about direct deposit or the ETA, contact your regional paying agency or financial institution, call 202-874-6590 or visit the Department of Treasury Web site at *www.fms.treas.gov/eft*.

—Survivors Benefits—

Losing your spouse is difficult enough without having to worry about how you are going to get by financially. Social Security survivors benefits can help. When a person dies, certain members of the family may be eligible for survivors benefits if the deceased worked, paid Social Security taxes and earned enough credits, no matter at what age he or she died. The number of credits needed depends on their age at the time of death. The younger a person is, the fewer credits are needed to be eligible for survivors benefits. However, nobody needs more than 40 credits (10 years of work) to be eligible for any Social Security benefits.

Who Are the Survivors?

Social Security survivors benefits can be paid to:

- A widow/widower: full benefits at full retirement age (currently age 65), or reduced benefits as early as age 60. A disabled widow/widower may receive benefits as early as age 50.
- A widow/widower at any age, if he or she takes care of the deceased's child, under age 16, or disabled, who receives Social Security benefits.
- Unmarried children under 18 or up to age 19 if they are attending elementary or secondary school full-time. A child is eligible to receive benefits at any age if he or she was disabled before age 22 and remains disabled. Under certain circumstances, benefits also can be paid to stepchildren, grandchildren or adopted children.
- Dependent parents at 62 or older.

 SAVVY NOTE: Full retirement age for surviving spouses will gradually increase from 65 to 67. See the Age Scale on page 190.

How Much Do Survivors Get?

The amount of the survivors benefit is based on the earnings of the person who died. The more the worker paid into Social Security, the higher the benefits will be. The amount a survivor receives is a percentage of the deceased's basic Social Security benefit. Here is a savvy breakdown of the most typical situations:

- Widow or widower at full retirement age or older, 100 percent
- Widow or widower age 60–64, about 71–94 percent
- Widow or widower at any age with a child under age 16, 75 percent
- Children, 75 percent

 SAVVY NOTE: If a person is receiving widow/widower's benefits, they can switch to their own retirement benefits (assuming they are eligible and their retirement rate is higher than the widow/widower's rate) as early as age 62. In many cases, a widow/widower can begin receiving one benefit at a reduced rate and then switch to the other benefit at an unreduced rate at full retirement age. However, they will not be paid both benefits: They will be paid the higher of the two benefits.

SAVVY TIP: If you work, depending on your income, your survivors benefits could be affected. See how work affects your benefits on page 199.

Divorced Survivor

You may also be interested to know that a former spouse can receive benefits under the same circumstances as a widow/widower if the marriage lasted 10 years or more. Benefits paid to a surviving divorced spouse who is 60 or older will not affect the benefit rates for other survivors receiving benefits.

SAVVY NOTE: In general, a widow/widower is not eligible to receive benefits if he/she remarries before the age of 60 (50 if disabled) unless the latter marriage ends, whether by death, divorce or annulment. However, remarriage after age 60 (50 if disabled) will not prevent payments on a former spouse's record.

To file for benefits, or for more information, call Social Security at 1-800-772-1213 or visit *www.socialsecurity.gov.* Social Security offers a free booklet called "Survivors Benefits," publication no. 05-10084, or you can see it online at *www.sss.gov/pubs/10084/html.*

— Divorced Benefits —

If you were married 9 years, 11 months and 27 days, you are *not* eligible for divorced Social Security benefits. But if you were married 10 years (or more), you might be!

Divorced spouses are eligible to receive benefits on a former husband's or wife's Social Security record if the marriage lasted at least 10 years and the ex-spouse is

- At least 62,
- Unmarried, and
- Not eligible for an equal or higher benefit on his or her own record or someone else's Social Security record.

If the couple has been divorced at least two years, the spouse may receive benefits even if the worker is not retired. The two-year waiting period is waived if the worker received benefits before the divorce. Also, if the spouse marries, in most cases benefits will stop. But if the new marriage ends, benefits may be started again.

How Much Are Divorced Benefits?

The amount of your monthly Social Security payment will depend on your age when you start getting benefits.

- At full retirement age, 65 and 4 months in 2004 (see Social Security Age Scale on page 190), a divorced spouse can receive up to 50 percent of what their ex-spouse is entitled to at full retirement age.

- At age 62, a divorced spouse will receive a reduced benefit (around 37 percent or less) of what their ex-spouse is entitled to at full retirement age.

 SAVVY NOTE: The amount of benefits you receive as a divorced spouse does not affect the amount of benefits a current spouse may receive. In fact, unless you tell them, the ex-spouse won't even know you're receiving benefits on their record.

One Check per Person

If you're entitled to Social Security on your own record, you cannot collect benefits on both your and your ex-spouse's record—only the higher of the two benefits.

To Apply

If you file for divorced Social Security benefits, you'll need to give your ex-spouse's Social Security number. If you don't know the number, you'll need to provide your ex-spouse's date and place of birth and parents' names. For more information, call 1-800-772-1213 or visit *www.socialsecurity.gov*.

— Divorced Widows and Widowers Benefits —

Attention divorced widows and widowers! You may be long divorced, but you might be eligible for Social Security survivors benefits on your ex-spouse's record. The Social Security scoop on divorced widows or widowers is that if you are the unremarried, divorced spouse of a worker who dies, you may get benefits just the same as a widow or widower, provided that your marriage lasted 10 years or more. But if you remarry before reaching age 60 (50 if disabled), you cannot receive benefits as long as the marriage remains in effect.

 SAVVY NOTE: Widows and widowers may begin receiving benefits if they are age 60 or older (50 if you are disabled).

Monthly Amount

The amount of your monthly Social Security payment will depend on the age when you start getting benefits. It also will depend on the amount your deceased ex-spouse would have been entitled to, or was receiving, when he or she died.

Widows and widowers benefits range from 71.5 percent of the deceased ex-spouse's benefit amount, if they begin at age 60, to 100 percent if they begin at age 65. So, if you start receiving benefits at age 65, you'll get 100 percent of the amount your ex-spouse would be receiving if he or she were still alive.

 SAVVY NOTE: Starting in 2005, the age at which the 100 percent widows and widowers benefits are payable will increase gradually until it reaches age 66 in 2011 and 67 in 2029 (see the Age Scale on page 190).

One Check per Person

You cannot collect Social Security benefits on both your and your ex-spouse's records—only the higher of the two.

Good to Know

- If you are entitled to retirement benefits on your own work record, you are eligible to take reduced retirement payments at age 62 and then receive full widows or widowers benefits at age 65.
- If you are eligible for benefits on your own work record, you may want to take reduced widows or widowers benefits until you are age 65 and file a claim for retirement benefits on your own record.

If You Aren't Getting Social Security Benefits

If you are eligible, you should apply for survivor benefits promptly, because in some cases benefits may not be retroactive. You can apply by calling or visiting any Social Security office or by making an appointment: Call 1-800-772-1213.

If You're Already Getting Social Security Benefits

If you're getting benefits on your own record, you'll need to complete an application to get survivors benefits. You might be able to get more money as a widow or widower.

SAVVY NOTE: Additional rules apply to the Social Security survivors benefit process if you are disabled or are caring for your ex-spouse's child who is age 16 or under or is disabled. Be sure to visit with a Social Security representative to understand all your possible options, or call 1-800-772-1213.

—How Work Affects Social Security—

If you plan on working into your 60s, you might want to think twice about taking early Social Security retirement benefits. Many seniors today are working past age 62, thinking they will supplement their Social Security retirement—not realizing that what they might be supplementing is Uncle Sam. Here's the Social Security scoop on how work affects your benefits.

As of January 1, 2000, Social Security changed the way to determine how your benefits are affected when you work while receiving *retirement* or *survivors benefits*. When you're working, your benefit amount will now be reduced only until you reach your full retirement age (see the Social Security Age Scale on page 190), not up to age 70 as the previous law required.

SAVVY NOTE: A different set of rules applies to people receiving Social Security Disability benefits or Supplemental Security Income (SSI) payments. Also, a different set of rules applies to most work performed outside the United States.

Here's the Social Security formula to determine how much your benefit must be reduced:

- If you're under full retirement age when you begin receiving your Social Security benefits, $1 in benefits will be deducted for each $2 you earn above the annual limit. For 2004, that limit is $11,640.
- In the year you reach full retirement age (in 2004, age 65 and 4 months), $1 in benefits will be deducted for each $3 you earn above a different limit, but only for the months before the month you reach full retirement age. For 2004, this limit is $31,080. Starting with the month you reach full retirement age, you can receive your full benefits with no limit on your earnings.

Here are some savvy examples of how the rules would affect you:

- Let's say you begin receiving Social Security benefits at age 62 in January 2003, and you're entitled to $600 a month ($7,200 for the year). During the year, you work and earn $20,000 ($8,480 over the $11,520 limit). Of that, $4,240 would be withheld from your Social Security benefits ($1 for every $2 you earn over the limit), so you would receive $2,960 in benefits instead of $7,200.
- Or let's say you were age 64 at the beginning of 2004 (entitled to $1,000 a month Social Security benefits), but reached full retirement age (65 and 4 months) in August 2004. You earned $33,000 in the seven months from January through July. During this period, the amount of benefits withheld would be $640 ($1 for every $3 you earned above the $31,080 limit). You would still receive $6,360 of your Social Security benefits instead of $7,000 from the first seven months.

    And, starting in August (when you reach 65 and 4 months), you would begin receiving your full benefits, no matter how much you earn.

What Income Counts? . . . And When Does Social Security Count It?

If you work for someone else, only your wages count toward Social Security's earnings limits. If you're self-employed, only your net earnings from self-employment are counted. In either case, nonwork income such as other government benefits, investment earnings, interest, pensions, annuities and capital gains is not counted.

 SAVVY NOTE: This special first-year retirement rule is for people who retire in midyear and have already earned more than the yearly earnings limit before they retire. That's why there's a special rule that applies to earnings for the first year of retirement.

Reporting Changes in Your Earnings

Social Security calculated your benefit payments based on the earnings estimate you gave when you applied for Social Security or your most recent estimate of earnings. If at any time during the year you see that your earnings will be different from what you had estimated, you should call Social Security to revise your estimate.

Social Security Information

For more specific information, call Social Security at 1-800-772-1213 or visit *www .socialsecurity.gov.* Social Security also offers a free booklet called "How Work Affects Your Benefits," publication no. 05-10069, or you can see it online *www.ssa.gov/pubs/10069/ html.*

—Social Security Benefits and Taxes—

Sorry to break this to you, but depending on your income, your Social Security benefits might be taxable! However, this applies only if you have other substantial income, such as wages, self-employment, interest, dividends and other taxable income that you have to report on your tax return in addition to your benefits.

 SAVVY NOTE: No one pays taxes on more than 85 percent of his or her Social Security benefits.

Filing with the IRS

Here are the IRS income-tax rules on your Social Security benefits for 2004:

- If you file a federal tax return as an "individual" and your combined income is between $25,000 and $34,000, you may have to pay income tax on 50 percent of your Social Security benefits. If your combined income is above $34,000, up to 85 percent of your Social Security benefits are subject to income tax.
- If you file a joint return, you may have to pay taxes on 50 percent of your benefits if you and your spouse have a combined income that is between $32,000 and $44,000. If your combined income is more than $44,000, up to 85 percent of your Social Security benefits is subject to income tax.
- If you are married but file a separate tax return, you probably will pay taxes on your benefits.

 SAVVY NOTE: On your 1040 tax return, your "combined income" is the sum of your adjusted gross income plus nontaxable interest plus one-half of your Social Security benefits.

Every January you will receive a Social Security Benefit Statement (Form SSA-1099) showing the amount of benefits you received in the previous year. You can use this statement when you complete your federal income tax return to find out if your benefits are subject to tax.

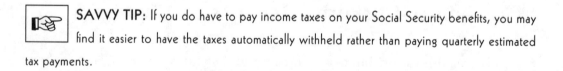 **SAVVY TIP:** If you do have to pay income taxes on your Social Security benefits, you may find it easier to have the taxes automatically withheld rather than paying quarterly estimated tax payments.

How to Have Federal Taxes Withheld from Your Social Security Benefits

Although you're not required to have federal taxes withheld from your Social Security benefits, you may find that easier than making out-of-pocket lump-sum payments.

To have your taxes withheld, you must

- Complete IRS Form W-4V (Voluntary Withholding Request).
- Select what percentage of your monthly benefit amount you want withheld: 7, 10, 15 or 27 percent. Only these percentages may be used. Flat dollar amounts are not acceptable.
- After you've made your selection, sign the form and return it to your local Social Security office by mail or in person. To get the address of your local Social Security office, call 1-800-772-1213 or visit *www.socialsecurity.gov*.

If you want to know how much a particular percentage is equal to in dollars, call Social Security at 1-800-772-1213. Also, if you have questions about your tax liability or want to request a Form W-4V, call the IRS at 1-800-829-3676.

 SAVVY NOTE: Each time you want to change your withholding (or stop the withholding), you will need to complete the form and send it to Social Security.

—Social Security Disability—

Disability is one of those things you may hear about in the news but not think of as something that might happen to you. The chances of becoming disabled are probably greater than you realize. Studies show that a 20-year-old worker has a 3-in-10 chance of becoming disabled before reaching retirement age.

If you become disabled and can't work anymore, Social Security can provide valuable help to you. Here's what you should know.

Defining Disability

The first thing to keep in mind is this: With Social Security there is no such thing as a partial disability or a short-term disability. It's not like Workers' Compensation, where they have all manner of categories including temporary, partial and permanent partial disability. You're either disabled long term or you're not, and if not long term, the disability must be expected to last at least one year or to result in death.

Five Steps

There are five questions that Social Security will ask about your disability in order to assess your eligibility for benefits. They are

- Are you still working? If you are, and making some money, generally you are not considered disabled.
- Is your condition severe? That means, does it interfere with your ability to do basic work-related activities? Keep in mind that under the Americans with Disabilities legislation, companies are doing more and more to accommodate disabled workers, and most companies don't want to lose good workers, even if it means they have to change a person's workstation or job assignment to keep them.
- Is your condition on Social Security's list of disabling impairments? There are far too many of them to discuss here, but if your condition is listed, you may be automatically eligible for benefits. If it's not on the list, don't despair. It just means that Social Security will investigate your claim on an individual, case-by-case basis. And keep in mind that disability can cover a range of mental and psychiatric disorders too.
- Can you do the same work you previously did? If so, your claim will be denied.
- Can you do some other type of work? If you are paralyzed from the waist down, for example, you may no longer be able to do your original job, but you may be able to do office work or some other tasks that will keep you employed with the same company.

The place to begin is with Social Security. Simply call them at 1-800-772-1213 and ask for an appointment, or go to your local Social Security office. Bring all your appropriate medical and personal paperwork to expedite your case. You'll also need the names and numbers of doctors, clinics and hospitals that treated you, their diagnoses and a list of medications you may be on as well as any other key medical records, including laboratory tests. Also, bring in work records, such as wage and tax information presented by your employer, to verify your work history.

 SAVVY TIP: If your injury was work-related, you may file for Social Security disability benefits while still receiving Workers' Compensation benefits. Workers' Comp benefits can reduce your Social Security benefits, or vice versa, depending on the rules in the state where you live, but in most cases there will be some additional federal payment. The Social Security Web site has calculators, at *www.ssa.gov/planners/calculators.htm,* that can give you a rough outline of your expected benefits based on your income history. For more information on Social Security Disability, visit *www.socialsecurity.gov* or call 1-800-722-1213.

SAVVY RESOURCE

- Social Security offers a free booklet called "Disability Benefits," publication no. 05-10029, or you can see it online at *www.ssa.gov/pubs/10029/html.*

—Social Security Appeals—

Do you have a disagreement with Uncle Sam? If so, you're not alone. Hundreds of thousands of people challenge rulings on their Social Security or Supplemental Security Income each year—so many, in fact, that there is an Office of Hearings and Appeals (OHA) dedicated to handling these cases.

 SAVVY NOTE: One thing we all should remember about Social Security or any other federal money is this: It's our money! We earned it!

Social Security Appeals Process

The first thing you should know is that if the Social Security Administration decides that you are not eligible or that the amount of your payment should change, they will send you a letter announcing their decision. Keep in mind that the "average" payment for a retired worker in 2004 is $922 a month, and the average disability benefit is $862, but it goes up for top income earners.

If you are unhappy with this initial decision, you have 60 days to file an appeal and your nearest Social Security office can help you with that letter. Or, they can help you fill out what is known as a Form 561, which also triggers what is called a reconsideration.

At this level, people who were not involved in the original decision will look at all the evidence presented in the original case, as well as any new information you may have, and then render a decision. The person who filed the appeal does not have to be present at this stage.

If you disagree with that ruling, then you have the right to ask for a hearing. At this level, one of Social Security's Administrative Law Judges—again, someone with no role in the earlier decisions—will hold a hearing. You have a right to be present with witnesses and will be notified of the time and place of the hearing. You also have the right to bring an attorney to this hearing. These hearings are usually held within an hour or two driving time of a person's home so the inconvenience is minor. Be prepared for the judge to ask questions of all parties, including the witnesses, but don't expect an immediate decision. This, too, will come in the mail.

The third step, if you're still dissatisfied, is to go to the Social Security Appeals Council. They can examine the case and render a decision themselves, or they can refer it back to another Administrative Law Judge for a review.

Now you're thinking, "Three strikes and you're out!" Right? Well, not quite.

The fourth and final step is to file a lawsuit in a federal district court and ask a federal judge who is not affiliated with the Social Security Administration for a ruling. Hopefully, that won't be necessary. And remember that there are attorneys who specialize in these kinds of claims. They may be brought in at any step in the process, but most charge a fee, which means if you don't win you could be out even more money.

Always, when battling city hall or any other government agency, arm yourself with information first. Start with the Social Security Administration itself and its Office of Hearings and Appeals. For more information call Social Security at 1-800-772-1213 or visit *www.socialsecurity.gov*. Social Security also offers a free booklet called "The Appeals Process," publication no. 05-10041, or you can see it online at *www.ssa.gov/pubs/10041/html*.

—SSI—

Have you heard about SSI? No, it doesn't stand for "savvy senior information." It's an acronym for Supplemental Security Income, a program run by Social Security.

Am I Eligible?

If you get SSI, you usually get food stamps and Medicaid too. Medicaid helps pay doctor and hospital bills. To get SSI, you must be elderly or blind or have a disability.

- Elderly means you are 65 or older.
- Blind means you are either totally blind or have very poor eyesight. Children as well as adults can get benefits because of blindness.
- Disability means you have a physical or mental problem that is expected to last at least a year or result in death. Children as well as adults can get benefits because of disability.

How Much Can You Get from SSI?

The federal standard monthly SSI check is the same in all states:

- $564 for one person in 2004; or
- $846 for a couple.

SAVVY NOTE: Not everyone gets this exact amount. You may get more if you live in a state that adds to the SSI check. Or you may get less if you or your family have other money coming in each month. Your living arrangements also make a difference in eligibility and the amount you can get.

Things You Own and Your Income

To get SSI, the things you own and your income must be below certain amounts. Social Security does not count everything you own when deciding if you can get SSI. For example, they don't count your home and they usually don't count your car. However, they do count cash, bank accounts, stocks and bonds. You may be able to get SSI if the things they count are no more than:

- $2,000 for one person; or
- $3,000 for a couple.

Your Income

Your income includes earnings, Social Security payments, pensions and noncash items you receive, such as food or shelter. The amount of income you can have each month and still get SSI depends on where you live and if you work or not. In some states you can have more income than in others.

For detailed SSI income information, or to sign up for SSI, call Social Security at 1-800-772-1213 or visit *www.socialsecurity.gov*. Social Security offers a free booklet called "Supplemental Security Income," publication no. 05-11000, or you can see it online at *www.ssa.gov/pubs/11000/html*.

— Notch Notes —

Those who are "notch babies" (people born between 1917 and 1921), beware! There are still fund-raising groups out there that solicit money from people (whom they call victims) born during the 1917–1926 period. They send out letters asking people to sign petitions to Congress and enclose a check. They stir up resentment and tell people they're being discriminated against based on the year they were born. *Don't send your money!*

What Are Notch Babies?

Notch babies are people born between 1917 and 1921 who receive Social Security benefits calculated using a different formula from the one used for people born before or after that time.

 SAVVY NOTE: Many people think the notch years are 1917 to 1926. This is not correct!

Why Are There Notch Babies?

The reason for the notch baby dilemma began back in 1972, when Congress enacted changes to the Social Security law that established annual cost-of-living (COLA) increases in Social Security benefits. The formula that was set by law was flawed and actually paid too much to beneficiaries, and if this were left uncorrected, the system would be at risk for going bankrupt (which doesn't bode well for you and me). The law was therefore changed in 1977 to fix the formula, but by that time, many people born between 1910 and 1916 had already retired and had their benefits calculated using the incorrect formula. Congress, in a compassionate move, opted not to take anything away from those retirees. Therefore, those people are receiving additional money. Congress, in another compassionate move, also was concerned about the impact of this change on people about to retire, so a special "transition" formula was created for people who were within five years of retirement age when the law was changed.

Three Social Security Classes

There are three "classes" of Social Security beneficiaries:

- Benefits for people born before 1917 are calculated under the incorrect 1972 formula, so they are actually getting a windfall (additional money), compared to the original intent of Congress.
- People born between 1917 and 1921 are paid the benefits calculated using either the correct 1977 formula or the transition formula, whichever is higher.
- The rest of us! People born after 1921, who have their benefits calculated using the correct 1977 formula.

Notch Fund-raising

The major notch fund-raiser today is the Retired Enlisted Association (TREA) Senior Citizens League in Washington, D.C. In its view, the notch extends to people born as late as 1926, which nicely extends its mailing list. The notch is a nifty fund-raiser for legislators too. By introducing or cosponsoring a bill, they can pick up a campaign contribution from TREA. The current bills ask for a flat $5,000 settlement for everyone in the notch.

SAVVY NOTE: I recommend you don't waste your money on "notch reform legislation" because it will never pass! Also, you might be interested to know that in 1992 Congress appointed a commission to study the notch. It reported, in 1994, that no injustice had been done.

FINANCES

FINANCES, OR RATHER THE LACK OF FINANCES, IS ONE OF THE BIGGEST concerns of seniors as they head toward retirement. Will I have enough? What will I do if I run out? What about insurance?

In this section, *The Savvy Senior* offers insight on topics such as financial retirement, IRAs and 401(k) options. We also take a look at such senior considerations as health-insurance options should you retire early or lose your job, long-term-care insurance, reverse mortgages, wills and trusts and what to do should you get into debt. *The Savvy Senior* will also tell you about a host of programs that can help you save money and assist you in planning your financial future.

—Financial Tips for Retirement—

The average American spends around 18 years in retirement. Only about half of the people approaching retirement have any idea how much they need to save for their retirement years. Is this you? If so, don't fret! It's never too late to start a savvy retirement plan, but don't put it off any longer—START NOW.

To live well in retirement, you no longer can rely solely on Social Security or a company pension plan. Instead, you will have to depend on how skillfully you plan and invest, and whether you make good use of tax-advantaged savings plans such as 401(k)s and IRAs.

Here are some savvy tips to help you develop your financial retirement plan:

- **Know your retirement needs:** Retirement is expensive! Some experts estimate that you'll need about 70 percent of your preretirement income to maintain your standard of living when you stop working. That might be enough if you've paid off your mortgage and are in excellent health. But if you plan to build your dream house, trot around the globe or play golf every day at Pebble Beach, you may need 100 percent of your income or more. Remember, too, that your health-care expenses are likely to go up in retirement, if only because you'll be paying more for insurance.

 SAVVY TIP: Be out of debt before you retire!

- **Find out about your Social Security benefits:** Social Security pays the average retiree about 40 percent of preretirement earnings. If you haven't already received a statement in the mail, you may call the Social Security Administration at 1-800-772-1213 for a free Personal Earnings and Benefit Estimate Statement or use their online calculator to make estimates based on expected earnings.
- **Learn about your employer's pension or profit-sharing plan:** If your employer offers a plan, check to see what your benefit is worth. Most employers will

provide an individual benefit statement if you request one. Before you change jobs, find out what will happen to your pension. Learn what benefits you may have from previous employment. Find out if you will be entitled to benefits from your spouse's plan.

- **Contribute to a tax-sheltered savings plan:** If your employer offers a tax-sheltered savings plan, such as a 401(k), sign up and contribute all you can. Your taxes will be lower, your company may kick in more and automatic deductions make it easy. Over time, compound interest and tax deferrals make a big difference in the amount of money you will accumulate.

- **Put your money into an Individual Retirement Account (IRA):** In 2004, you can put up to $3,000 a year into an Individual Retirement Account (IRA) ($3,500 the year you turn age 50 and over) and gain tax advantages. In 2005, that goes up to $4,000, and $4,500 age 50 and over. When you open an IRA, you have two options: a traditional IRA or the Roth IRA. The tax treatment of your contributions and withdrawals will depend on which option you select. Also, you should know that the after-tax value of your withdrawal will depend on inflation and the type of IRA you choose.

- **Don't touch your savings:** Don't dip into your retirement savings. You'll lose principal and interest and you may lose tax benefits. If you change jobs, roll over your savings directly into an IRA or your new employer's retirement plan.

SAVVY TIP: You can count on needing at least $15 to $20 in investment savings to cover each dollar you will need for your retirement income. For example, if you need $20,000 investment income to supplement your Social Security and pension, you will need a nest egg of $300,000 to $400,000.

- **Consider basic investment principles:** How you save can be as important as how much you save. Inflation and the type of investment you make play important roles in how much you'll have saved at retirement. Know how your pension or savings plan is invested. Financial security and knowledge go hand in hand.

SAVVY RESOURCES

- The National "Save For Your Future" Campaign: a partnership between the Social Security Administration and the American Savings Education Council committed to informing Americans about the need to save and plan for retirement and other life stages. Visit *www.saveforyourfuture.org.*
- Certified Financial Planner Board of Standards: *www.cfp-board.org.*
- Consumer Federation of America: *www.consumerfed.org.*
- Federal Consumer Information Center: *www.pueblo.gsa.gov.*
- American Savings Education Council: *www.asec.org.*
- Pension and Welfare Benefits Administration: *www.dol.gov/ebsa.*
- U.S. Securities and Exchange Commission: *www.sec.gov.*

—Choosing a Financial Planner—

With the erosion of retirement savings over the last few years, lots of older Americans are out looking for savvy professional financial advice.

Professional Financial Planner

What you can expect from a professional financial planner is someone who will help you see a clear "big picture" of your current financial situation and will help you make good financial planning decisions that are right for you and your situation.

 SAVVY TIP: Certified Financial Planner or CFP is a recommended mark of quality when choosing a financial planner.

Nationally there are more than 40,000 certified financial planners (CFPs), but there are also many other types of advisers—for example, insurance salespeople, brokers and bankers—who offer financial planning and advice but don't always have appropriate certification. Here are some considerations to help you better prepare for your financial planning experience and assist your search for the right financial whiz.

How to Make Financial Planning Work for You

- Set measurable financial goals: Set specific goals that you want to achieve and decide when you want to reach them. For example, instead of saying you want to be "comfortable" when you retire, quantify what "comfortable" means, so that you'll know when you've reached your goal.
- Understand the effect of each financial decision: Each financial decision you make can affect several other areas of your life. For example, an investment decision may have tax consequences that are harmful to your estate plans.
- Be realistic in your expectations: Remember that events beyond your financial planner's control, such as inflation or changes in the stock market or interest rates, will affect your financial planning results.
- Reevaluate your financial situation: Revisit and revise your financial plan as time goes by to assure you stay on track with your long-term goals.
- You are in charge: Provide the planner with all of the relevant information on your financial situation. Ask questions about the recommendations offered to you and play an active role in decision making.

The Search

Here are 10 good questions from the CFP Board of Standards that will help you interview and evaluate several financial planners to find the one that's right for you. You will want to select a competent, qualified professional with whom you feel comfortable and one whose business style suits your specific needs.

- **What experience do you have?** Choose a financial planner with at least three years' experience.
- **What are your qualifications?** The term *financial planner* is used by many financial professionals. Find out their educational background and certifications.

- **What services do you offer?** The services a financial planner offers depend on a number of factors, including credentials, licenses and areas of expertise.
- **What is your approach to financial planning?** Ask the financial planner about the types of clients and financial situations he or she typically likes to work with.
- **Will you be the only person working with me?** The financial planner may be the only one to work with you, may have others in the office assist him or her or may be part of a team.
- **How will I pay for your services?** The financial planner should clearly state in writing how he or she will be paid for the services: usually by fees, commissions or both.
- **How much do you typically charge?** The financial planner should be able to provide you with an estimate of possible costs based on the work to be performed.
- **Could anyone besides me benefit from your recommendations?** Ask the planner to provide you with a description of his or her conflicts of interest in writing.
- **Have you ever been publicly disciplined for any unlawful or unethical actions in your professional career?** Ask what organizations the planner is regulated by, and contact these groups to conduct a background check.
- **Can I have it in writing?** Ask the planner to provide you with a written agreement that details the services that will be provided.

SAVVY RESOURCES

- Certified Financial Planner Board of Standards: Provides access to and benefits from competent financial planning. Call 1-888-237-6275 or visit *www.cfp-board.org.*
- National Association of Personal Financial Advisors: the largest professional association of comprehensive, fee-only financial planners in the United States. Call 1-888-333-6659 or visit *www.napfa.org.*
- Financial Planning Association: Call 1-800-647-6340 or visit *www.fpanet.org.*

—401(k) Retirement Options—

There are many different options for 401(k) withdrawals. Every situation is different, but one common thread that seems to run through the list of things people are looking to achieve is stretching their money as far as possible, without paying high taxes.

 SAVVY NOTE: Talk to a qualified tax adviser or financial planner to review your options before making any decisions affecting your 401(k).

401(k) Options

The withdrawal or distribution options your employer offers depend on the rules for your company's plan. Here are some of the possibilities:

- Leaving the money in the plan
- Cashing out in a lump sum
- Rolling over a lump sum into an IRA
- Converting to an annuity
- Taking the money in installments
- Using some combination of these

In deciding on a withdrawal plan, you'll have to weigh such factors as your age, other sources of income, your tax situation and how comfortable you feel investing and managing your money. Here's the breakdown of possible 401(k) considerations.

- **Stay put:** Your company may allow you to leave money in the 401(k) plan and withdraw it later. When you turn 70½, however, the IRS requires you to start taking the money out or pay a stiff penalty if you don't. This option is most attractive if you don't need the money immediately, because it enables you to stay with investments with which you're familiar and comfortable; however, the downside is that your investment choices will be limited to those in the 401(k) plan.

- **Cash out:** You can choose to take a "lump-sum distribution" by cashing out your account. Beware: This is a very tempting option because the cash can be invested or spent. IRS ALERT: Know that if you choose the lump-sum cash-out you'll have to pay income tax on the money you withdraw, and the IRS requires your employer to withhold 20 percent of the lump sum toward that income tax.

 SAVVY NOTE: If you're younger than 55, you will have to pay an additional 10 percent penalty for early withdrawal.

- **IRA rollover:** To keep from paying high taxes, a savvy alternative is to roll over the lump sum into a traditional IRA at a mutual fund company, stock brokerage, bank, credit union or other financial institution. The great advantage of a rollover is flexibility, because you can invest IRA money in stocks, bonds, mutual funds, CDs, treasury notes or other instruments and sell them at any time.

 SAVVY TIP: To avoid income tax and penalties, the rollover must be completed within 60 days of the withdrawal from your plan.

- **Annuities:** About 30 percent of plans allow you to convert some or all of your 401(k) assets into an annuity that guarantees regular fixed payments. An annuity can provide you guaranteed income for the rest of your life and relieve you of the challenge of managing your investments. Annuities come in many forms and options. Choose carefully!

 SAVVY NOTE: When you convert to an annuity, your 401(k) principal is, in most cases, no longer available to you after you start receiving payments.

- **Installments:** Some employers allow you to withdraw a percentage of the assets from your 401(k) in installments, most commonly over 5, 10 or 15 years. If you're happy keeping your savings in your employer's plan and want a steady stream of income but don't want to be locked into the rules of an annuity, this approach could be right for you; however, the down side is that you will have fewer investment choices and less flexibility.

- **Combination:** You can combine the above options for withdrawing your 401(k) money. This approach enables you to tailor a plan best suited to your needs.

This information was obtained in part from the AARP.

SAVVY RESOURCES

- Internal Revenue Service: *www.irs.gov*.
- Federal Government Consumer Information Center: Offers free pamphlets on investing, saving and retirement planning including 401(k) plans and annuities. Call 1-888-878-3256 or visit *www.pueblo.gsa.gov*.
- Financial Planning Association: Call 1-800-322-4237 or visit *www.fpanet.org*.

— IRA Savvy —

Many people get confused about the age that they're required to start withdrawing from their traditional IRA. The magic age is **70½**, when you're required to take a minimum withdrawal. And if you don't take your required IRA distribution, or if you take one that is too small, you'll be taxed at a whopping 50 percent rate on the amount that should have been withdrawn but wasn't, and then you still have to take out the correct amount of the distribution and pay tax on it too.

 SAVVY NOTE: If you have a Roth IRA, the IRS does not require you to make a minimum withdrawal.

Why 70½?

If you turn 70 in 2004 and your birthday is between January and June, that means you will be 70½ and must take a distribution for this year. However, if you turn 70 in 2004 and your birthday is between July and December, then you won't be 70½ until 2005, and that is when you must take your first distribution. Got it? Wait, there is more! If 2004 is the first year for your mandatory distribution, then you have a choice of taking it during the 2004 calendar year or waiting until as late as April 1, 2005. If you wait to take the 2004 distribution until 2005, then you will have to take the 2005 distribution as well as 2004's (this April 1 option to wait applies only to the first distribution year).

 SAVVY NOTE: It's best to take the 2004 distribution in 2004 and the 2005 distribution in 2005. It only makes sense to wait and double up the next year if your income will substantially fall in that year and the tax savings will be worth it. You should consult with your tax adviser about this option.

How Much Do I Have to Withdraw?

The formula for figuring this out starts by taking the December 31 value of your IRA and dividing it by a factor from Uncle Sam's Life Expectancy Table or the Minimum Distribution Incidental Benefit Table.

SAVVY NOTE: Talk to your IRA custodian for details on the Life Expectancy Table or the Minimum Distribution Incidental Benefit Table.

Here's an example: Let's say that your traditional IRA account is worth $100,000 on December 31, 2004, and your life expectancy is 10 years. You should withdraw $10,000 from your traditional IRA account in 2005. (The $100,000 IRA divided by your 10-year life expectancy equals $10,000.) Your minimum withdrawal will change every year as your account balance and your life expectancy change. Consult with your IRA custodian for a detailed breakdown.

SAVVY NOTE: If your spouse is 10 years younger, the actual joint life expectancy can be used, which will make the minimum distribution smaller.

Multiple IRAs

If you have more than one IRA or IRAs at different custodians, figure out the minimum amount for each IRA and then choose which one(s) to withdraw from. You don't have to take a little from each IRA. The government cares only that you take out the correct amount, and you can take it anytime during the year.

Securities

If you own securities in your IRA, most custodians at brokerage firms will allow you to take out shares equal to the amount of the minimum distribution instead of selling the security and taking out cash. If you have your custodian withhold taxes from the distribution, then cash must be taken for that portion, but if you elect no tax withholding, then you can move your whole distribution in securities. This is called a *like kind* distribution. Call your IRA custodian and ask them for the details.

Taking IRA Distributions Before Age 59½

Remember that you can't take distributions from your IRA balance until you are age 59½ without paying a 10 percent penalty. However, there are a few exceptions in which you can avoid the penalty (although ordinary income taxes are still due on traditional IRA distributions):

- In the case of death, disability or first-time home ownership
- Where you decide to "annuitize" your IRA in substantially equal annual payments calculated over your life expectancy (or the joint life expectancy of you and a beneficiary) before age 59½
- The use of IRA distributions to pay deductible medical expenses that exceed 7.5 percent of your adjusted gross income (AGI)
- The use of IRA distributions to pay qualified higher education expenses

- Internal Revenue Service (IRS): You may order IRS Publication 590: "Individual Retirement Arrangements" by calling 1-800-829-3676, or read it online at *www.irs.gov.*
- AARP Financial Planning Page: resource page on retirement income at *www.aarp.org/financial.*

—Health-Insurance Options Before Medicare—

Health insurance is a big reason many seniors don't retire before age 65, the year they become eligible for Medicare. If you do decide to retire early or if you unexpectedly lose your job, don't worry, you do have some health-insurance options. Here are a few to consider.

Your Former Employer

Medical coverage from your former employer is probably your best option. If your company offers continuing health coverage, do it! But be sure to check for any changes in coverage, like deductible increases or service decreases. You also may have to pay a monthly premium that's higher than the one you were paying while you were working.

COBRA

If your employer doesn't offer medical insurance, look next to what is known as the Consolidated Omnibus Budget Reconciliation Act, also known as COBRA. This is a law—not an insurance policy—requiring qualified employers with group health plans (and this includes most major corporations) to allow employees to continue under the group health-care plan if they retire or have been laid off or fired.

But there is a lot to consider, including

- Part of the premium paid by the employer will now be shifted to the employee, so be prepared for a jolt to the pocketbook. Sometimes companies pay 70, 80 and even 90 percent of an employee's health insurance while he or she is working. Depending on your situation (are your children and your spouse covered under your plan or another plan?), now that you are not working, your costs could be hundreds of dollars each month.
- It will be more expensive than you were used to paying, but it is likely to be less expensive than trying to pay for health care on your own or buying a policy privately.
- It can carry people for 18 months.
- Small employer plans (for companies with 20 or fewer employees) are generally exempt.

To apply for COBRA, your employer must notify your health-insurance company within 14 days of your removal from the payroll. Your employer or health-insurance company then must send you information about your COBRA rights within 30 days. You should receive information on how to apply for coverage, how much you will have to pay and how to pay. You can still get medical attention while your COBRA forms are being processed by your employer or the insurance company, because COBRA will cover you back to the date you left the payroll.

 SAVVY TIP: A good place to begin is at *www.cobrainsurance.com*.

Short-Term Insurance

Another option to consider is short-term medical insurance. These are policies offered by insurance companies for people who are temporarily in need. The duration of the policies varies from insurance provider to insurance provider, but many set limits from one to six months. There may be exceptions: They might not cover pre-existing conditions, for example, or routine matters such as annual exams and immunizations, but they might cover a catastrophic event such as a heart attack, which could wipe out 30 years of savings.

You can buy some policies in one-month increments, but keep in mind the fact that they can cancel you at the end of the month, particularly if you're filing a lot of medical claims. And any condition that appeared last month might be listed as a preexisting condition when you re-up the following month. I've heard it characterized as an insurance that will pay for any illness or injury suffered for the first time. As with any insurance, there is a host of limits and conditions to consider.

SAVVY TIP: The best thing to do is talk to your insurance provider, or shop around, comparing companies and multiple types of coverage before making any decision. Many Web sites can even quote rates, depending on a whole host of factors.

SAVVY RESOURCES

- Quotesmith.com: a great resource for insurance shopping and price comparing. Visit *www.quotesmith.com*.
- Health Insurance Association of America (HIAA): For consumer information, call 1-202-824-1600 or visit *www.hiaa.org*.

—Senior Legal Services—

Do you ever have legal questions you'd like answered or need advice on your estate planning, will or trust? If so, there are several great sources out there that offer legal advice and services to senior citizens and caregivers that are either free or discounted.

Each year under the Older Americans Act, the federal government distributes some of your tax dollars to the states to provide various services to seniors, one of which includes legal services for the elderly. How each state goes about providing the legal services will vary depending on funding. Here's a breakdown of four great legal programs that every senior should know about.

Legal Hotlines

Every state offers some type of legal hotline service, but there are currently 23 states including the District of Columbia that offer a program called "Senior Legal Hotlines," where all seniors over age 60 have access to free legal telephone advice, where they can speak with an attorney about their legal questions or problems.

The Senior Legal Hotlines are staffed with attorneys admitted to the bar of that state so all professional standards apply. The hotlines carry malpractice insurance and the service is limited to phone advice; however, some of the hotlines will do brief services such as review a document or write a simple letter on your behalf. Senior hotline services will also make referrals to help you get the appropriate assistance you need. For more information on Senior Legal Hotlines and to locate the toll-free number in your state, visit *www.legalhotlines.org*. This site also offers a state-by-state Legal Hotline Directory that lists all nonprofit organizations offering legal advice.

Legal Services for the Elderly

Coordinated by the Administration on Aging, Legal Services for the Elderly offers free legal advice, legal assistance or access to legal representation for people over the age of 60. To get more information on what programs are available in your community, contact your Area Aging Agency. Call your Eldercare Locator at 1-800-677-1116 to get the phone number of your local Aging Agency.

Legal Services

Directed by the Legal Services Corporation, Legal Services (also known as Legal Aid) offers free legal assistance to financially eligible people of all ages. Legal service programs are available nationwide, but each community program will differ in the services offered and income qualifications. For more information or to find the legal assistance program in your area, visit *www.lsc.gov* and click on "get legal assistance" or call the Legal Service Corporation at 1-202-295-1500.

AARP Legal Services Network

If you're a member of AARP, you are eligible for the Legal Services Network (LSN) program. This is a service that provides members a free 30-minute legal consultation with an attorney in their community who meets AARP standards. You can also receive some significant member discounts on other legal services you may need. For more information or to locate an attorney in your area, call 1-800-424-3410 or visit *www.aarp.org/lsn*.

SAVVY RESOURCES

- The American Bar Association (ABA): They offer a comprehensive state-by-state resource list on elder law services. Visit *www.abanet.org/aging* and click on "Find Legal Help in Your State."
- The National Academy of Elder Law Attorneys: They can help you find an attorney who specializes in working with older clients. Call 1-580-881-4005 or visit *www.naela.com*.

—Free Tax Preparation—

Looking for some extra savings at tax time? AARP can help!

Through the AARP Foundation program, and part of the National Community Service Program, AARP Tax-Aide is a free, confidential tax-preparation service that's been around since 1968. With over 8,500 sites nationwide, it is available to *all* taxpayers, middle- and low-income, with special attention to those 60 years and older.

 SAVVY NOTE: Since its inception, AARP Tax-Aide has helped more than 27 million individuals file their taxes.

Tax-Aide Service

AARP Tax-Aide volunteers are available to assist you from February 1 through April 15 at conveniently located sites such as libraries, malls, banks and senior centers. They will also visit taxpayers in their homes if they are physically unable to visit a site.

 SAVVY NOTE: Taxpayers with complex tax returns will be advised to seek professional tax assistance.

When you visit an AARP Tax-Aide site, you need to bring the following:

- Current year's tax forms and booklet
- Copy of last year's income-tax returns
- W-2 and W-2p forms from each employer, if you earned a salary
- Unemployment compensation statements
- SSA-1099 form if you were paid Social Security benefits
- All 1099 forms (1099-INT, 1099-DIV, 1099-misc, etc.) showing interest and/or dividends as well as documentation showing the original purchase price of your sold assets
- 1099R forms from the payer of your pension or annuity
- All forms indicating federal income tax paid
- Child-care provider information (name, employer ID, SSN)
- All receipts or canceled checks if itemizing deductions
- Social Security numbers for all dependents

Savvy Tax-Aide Volunteerism

Over 30,000 volunteers are what makes the AARP Tax-Aide program so successful. AARP constantly recruits volunteers to serve in a variety of rewarding positions. The only requirement for becoming a volunteer is a desire to give your time to help others.

AARP Tax-Aide volunteers receive comprehensive training in cooperation with the IRS. They also are reimbursed for their program-related, out-of-pocket expenses, including such costs as mileage, postage and basic supplies.

AARP Tax-Aide Contact Information

For more information about the AARP Tax-Aide service or to locate a site near you, call toll-free 1-888-AARPNOW (1-888-227-7669) or visit *www.aarp.org/ taxaide.*

SAVVY RESOURCES

Tax Counseling for the Elderly (TCE): The IRS also offers free tax counseling for seniors over 60 and voluntary income tax assistance (VITA) for younger people who need help. To find a site in your area, call your local IRS office or the national office at 1-800-829-1040.

—Get a Will—

Everybody needs a will. Yes, that means you! Without a will to indicate your wishes, the court will step in and distribute your property according to the laws of your state. Wills are not just for the rich. A will ensures your assets will be given to family members or other beneficiaries you designate.

 SAVVY NOTE: Forty percent of adults age 50 and older don't have wills.

What Happens If I Die Without a Will?

If you don't make a will or use some other legal method to transfer your property when you die, state law will determine what happens to your property. This process is called "intestate succession." Your property will be distributed to your spouse and children or, if you have neither, to other relatives according to a statutory formula. If no relatives can be found to inherit your property, it will go into your state's coffers.

Can I Do It Myself, or Do I Need a Lawyer?

Most people with uncomplicated family situations can create their own wills. For a will to be legal in most states, you have to be at least 18 years old and of sound mind. The document must be signed by you and witnessed by two people who won't receive anything from your estate. Basically, you just need to know what you own, whom you care about, and have a good self-help resource as a guide (available in bookstores, your public library or on the Internet). Still, it's wise to have an estate-planning attorney review your work and make sure everything is covered appropriately.

 SAVVY NOTE: Don't create your own will if you have a blended family or a complicated financial situation (property that is jointly owned) or if you have assets of more than $1 million. If these situations apply, see a lawyer who specializes in wills, trust and estates.

What Should I Include in My Will?

- Your name and place of residence
- A brief description of your assets
- Names of spouse, children and other beneficiaries, such as charities or friends
- Alternate beneficiaries, in the event a beneficiary dies before you do
- Specific gifts, such as an automobile or residence
- Establishment of trusts, if desired
- Cancellation of debts owed to you, if desired
- Name of an executor to manage the estate
- Name of a guardian for minor children
- Name of an alternative guardian, in the event your first choice is unable or unwilling to act
- Your signature
- Witnesses' signatures

SAVVY NOTE: An executor is the person who oversees the distribution of your assets in accordance with your will. Most people choose their spouse, an adult child, a relative, a friend or an attorney to fulfill this duty. If no executor is named in a will, a probate judge will appoint one.

Not a Tombstone

No matter how you write out your last will and testament, nothing is engraved in stone while you're alive. So if your circumstances change during your lifetime, you can always go back and modify your will however you want.

SAVVY RESOURCES

- Nolo Press self-help law center offers a savvy computer program called Will Maker that is relatively easy to use for the do-it-yourselfer: *www.nolo.com*.

- AARP Legal Services Network: *www.aarp.org/lsn*. AARP publishes the booklet "A Consumer's Guide to Living Trusts and Wills." For a free copy, send an e-mail to member@aarp.org with your name, mailing address and request, or log on to *www.aarp.org*.

- American Bar Association (ABA) publishes its *Guide to Wills and Estates*, which you may purchase for around $10 online at *www.abanet.org/abapubs*.

- American Academy of Estate Planning Attorneys: Call 1-800-846-1555 or visit *www.estateplanforyou.com*.

- MetLife Consumer Education Center: *www.lifeadvice.com*.

- National Network of Estate Planning Attorneys: Call 1-303-446-6100 or visit *www.netplanning.com/consumer*.

- National Academy of Elder Law Attorneys (NAELA), a membership association of attorneys who concentrate their practices on the legal issues of concern to older persons. Call 1-520-881-4005 or see their Web site at *www.naela.org*.

- National Association of Financial and Estate Planning: Call 1-801-266-9900 or visit *www.nafep.com*.

— Living Trusts —

If you're considering getting a living trust done, here are some simple answers to some basic questions you may not have known to ask.

A living trust, like a will, is a legal document that contains instructions for what you want to happen to your assets when you die. But unlike a will, a living trust avoids probate at death, can control all of your assets and can prevent the court from controlling your assets at incapacity.

What's the Scoop on Probate?

Probate is the legal process through which the court sees that, when you die, your debts are paid and your assets are distributed according to your will. If you don't have a valid will, your assets are distributed according to state law. The negative aspects of the probate legal process include

- Time, usually between nine months and two years.
- Legal expenses, ranging from 3 to 8 percent of the estate's value.
- Privacy: Probate is a public process, so any interested party can see what you owned and to whom you owed.

How Does a Living Trust Avoid Probate?

When you set up a living trust, you transfer assets from your name to the name of your trust, which you control. Legally you no longer own anything, but DON'T PANIC. Everything now belongs to your trust, so there is nothing for the courts to control when you die or become incapacitated.

Do I Lose Control of the Assets in My Trust?

NO! With a living trust you keep full control. As trustee of your trust, you can do anything you could do before: buy or sell assets, change or even cancel your trust. You even file the same tax returns. Nothing changes but the names on the titles.

How Do I Fund or Transfer My Assets into the Trust?

The attorney who sets up your trust can help you. You need to change titles on real estate and other titled assets (stocks, CDs, bank accounts, other investments, insurance, etc.). Most living trusts also include jewelry, art, furniture and other assets that do not have titles.

 SAVVY NOTE: Remember that simply writing a trust will not help you avoid probate. You must transfer your assets into your trust, or the trust isn't worth any more to you than the paper it's written on.

Who Should I Choose as a Trustee?

You may want your spouse, child, friend or professional trust manager as a trustee. It usually makes good sense to choose someone close to you.

What Is the Difference between a Revocable and Irrevocable Trust?

When you create a living trust, you must decide if it is revocable or irrevocable.

If the trust is revocable, you can modify it as you wish: You can change the beneficiaries, replace the trustee or end the trust entirely. If the trust is irrevocable, you can make no changes to its terms. If the trustee you name resigns, you may name a replacement trustee.

Trusts that are designed to avoid federal estate taxes are often drafted to be irrevocable while trusts designed only to avoid probate court frequently are revocable. You'll need to choose the one that best accomplishes what you want your trust to do.

Is a Living Trust Expensive?

How much you pay will depend on how complicated your plan is. Be sure to get estimates, but an average fee is between $1,000 and $2,000.

Should I Have an Attorney Do My Trust?

An attorney with savvy experience in living trusts can provide quality guidance. Using an attorney can be a wise decision.

If I Have a Living Trust, Do I Still Need a Will?

It's a good idea to have a "pour over" will, which acts as a safety net if you forget to transfer an asset to your trust. When you die, the will catches the forgotten asset and sends it into your trust.

What Are Supplemental and Special Needs Trusts?

Supplemental and Special Needs Trusts are trusts established to benefit a person with a disability by supplementing the government benefits they receive. With this kind of trust, a person such as a family member may establish a trust for a disabled individual without jeopardizing the beneficiary's eligibility for Medicaid and other government benefits.

Both types of trusts are irrevocable, and both are intended to provide a source of funds to augment government benefits received by a person with a disability. The primary difference between the Supplemental Trust and the Special Needs Trust is in whose money funds the trust. If the person with a disability is funding the trust with his or her own assets, such as through an inheritance or personal injury settlement, it is a Special Needs Trust. If the trust is funded with assets belonging to someone other than the person with a disability or his or her spouse, such as by a parent or grandparent, then it is a Supplemental Needs Trust.

Who Should Have a Living Trust?

If you own titled assets and want your loved ones (spouse, children or parents) to avoid court interference at your death or incapacity, you should consider a living trust.

SAVVY RESOURCES

- AARP Legal Services Network: *www.aarp.org/lsn*. AARP publishes the booklet "A Consumer's Guide to Living Trusts and Wills." For a free copy, send an e-mail to member@aarp.org with your name, mailing address and request, or log on to *www.aarp.org*.

- National Academy of Elder Law Attorneys (NAELA): a membership association of attorneys who concentrate their practices on the legal issues of concern to older persons. Call 1-520-881-4005 or visit their Web site at *www.naela* *.org*.

- National Network of Estate Planning Attorneys: Call 1-303-446-6100 or visit *www.netplanning.com/consumer*.
- The American Academy of Estate Planning Attorneys: Call 1-800-846-1555 or visit *www.aaepa.com*.
- National Association of Financial and Estate Planning: Call 1-801-266-9900 or visit *www.nafep.com*.

—Reverse Mortgages—

Nationwide, over 20 percent of seniors 65 and older live strictly on their Social Security retirement benefits. If you're feeling a financial pinch and are "house rich but cash poor," a reverse mortgage might be worth looking into.

Reverse Mortgage

A reverse mortgage is the opposite of a conventional mortgage and allows home-owners 62 and older who have paid off their mortgages, or have only small mortgage balances remaining, the opportunity to turn their home into a source of income by borrowing against the equity in it.

 SAVVY NOTE: The best candidates for these loans are retirees in their 70s or 80s.

Under a reverse mortgage, a lender advances an amount of money based on the value of the home to the current owner, either by making regular payments or issuing a lump sum payment. A lien is placed on the house, but the senior continues to own it. The lender is paid back the full amount of the loan plus interest when the senior moves permanently or dies.

Benefits

Reverse mortgage programs have several benefits. Being eligible is not dependent on income, and the payments will not affect Social Security or Medicare benefits because those programs are not based on financial need. However, eligibility for Supplemental Security Income, Medicaid, food stamps and other similar programs could be affected.

How Much You Get

The amount of cash you can get depends on your age, the value of the home and current interest rates. In general, the most cash goes to the oldest borrowers living in the homes of greatest value at a time when interest rates are low.

The amount of cash you can get also depends on the specific reverse mortgage plan or program you select. Available loan amounts vary greatly from one plan to another. Most homeowners get the largest cash advances from the federally insured Home Equity Conversion Mortgage (HECM).

Reverse mortgage loans can be paid to you all at once in a single lump sum of cash, as a regular monthly loan advance or as a line of credit, which lets you decide how much cash to use and when to use it. Or you may choose any combination of these payment plans.

What You Pay

The lowest-cost reverse mortgages are offered by state and local governments. They generally have low or no loan fees, and the interest rates are typically low or moderate as well. Private-sector reverse mortgages include a variety of costs. An application fee usually includes the cost of an appraisal and a credit report. Other loan costs typically include an origination fee, closing costs, insurance and a monthly servicing fee. These costs generally can be paid with loan advances, which mean they are added to your loan balance (the amount you owe). Interest is charged on all loan advances.

SAVVY NOTE: Reverse mortgages are most expensive in the early years of the loan, and then become less costly over time.

Types of Reverse Mortgages

There are three types of Reverse Mortgage plans. They vary according to their costs and terms. Here are some of the advantages and drawbacks of each type.

FHA-insured

This plan offers several options. You may receive monthly loan advances for a fixed term or for as long as you live in the home, a line of credit or monthly loan advances plus a line of credit. This reverse mortgage is not due as long as you live in your home. With the line-of-credit option, you may draw amounts as you need them over time. Closing costs, a mortgage-insurance premium and sometimes a monthly servicing fee are charged. Interest is charged at an adjustable rate on your loan balance; any interest rate changes do not affect the monthly payment, but rather how quickly the loan balance grows over time.

The FHA-insured reverse mortgage permits changes in payment options at little cost. This plan also protects you by guaranteeing that loan advances will continue to be made to you if a lender defaults. However, FHA-insured reverse mortgages may provide smaller loan advances than lender-insured plans. Also, FHA loan costs may be greater than uninsured plans.

Lender-insured

These reverse mortgages offer monthly loan advances or monthly loan advances plus a line of credit for as long as you live in your home. Interest may be assessed at a fixed rate or an adjustable rate, and additional loan costs can include a mortgage-insurance premium and other loan fees.

Loan advances from a lender-insured plan may be larger than those provided by FHA-insured plans. Lender-insured reverse mortgages may also allow you to mortgage less than the full value of your home, thus preserving home equity for later use by you or your heirs. However, these loans may involve greater loan costs than either FHA-insured or uninsured loans. Higher costs mean that your loan balance grows faster, leaving you with less equity over time.

Some lender-insured plans include an annuity that continues making monthly payments to you even if you sell your home and move. The security of these payments depends on the financial strength of the company providing them, so be sure to check the financial ratings of that company. Annuity payments may be taxable and affect your eligibility for Supplemental Security Income and Medicaid. These "reverse annuity mortgages" may also include additional charges based on increases in the value of your home during the term of your loan.

Uninsured

This reverse mortgage is dramatically different from FHA and lender-insured. An uninsured plan provides monthly loan advances for a fixed term only—a definite number of years that you select when you first take out the loan. Your loan balance becomes due and payable when the loan advances stop. Interest is usually set at a fixed interest rate and no mortgage insurance premium is required.

If you consider an uninsured reverse mortgage, think carefully about the amount of money you need monthly; how many years you may need the money; how you will repay the loan when it comes due; and how much remaining equity you will need after paying off the loan.

If you have short-term but substantial cash needs, the uninsured reverse mortgage can provide a greater monthly advance than the other plans. However, because you must pay back the loan by a specific date, it is important for you to have a source of repayment. If you are unable to repay the loan, you may have to sell your home and move.

SAVVY TIP: The FHA-insured Home Equity Conversion Mortgage (HECM) is the most well known and widely available reverse mortgage. It is backed by HUD, and can be used for any purpose. It is generally offered by mortgage companies or banks and is almost always the least-expensive private-sector reverse mortgage.

Things to Consider before Getting a Reverse Mortgage

- Determine if you really need a reverse mortgage or if another type of loan would be better for you. Depending upon your needs and your financial situation, you may be able to meet your goals with another, less costly financial solution than that provided by a reverse mortgage.

- See a HUD-approved reverse-mortgage counselor—free of charge—to help you decide if a reverse mortgage is for you, or to help you choose among the different types of reverse mortgages. Call 1-800-569-4287 to locate the HUD counseling agency nearest you.

- Shop around! Not all reverse mortgages are created equal. They vary substantially in how much cash you can get, what they cost and other features.

- Consider whether a reverse mortgage might make you ineligible for any public benefits you now receive or might otherwise receive in the future—for example, any "need-based" benefits such as Medicaid or Supplemental Social Security Income (SSI). Reverse mortgage payments will have to be structured so that monthly payments will be spent within the month they are received. If not, such payments will be considered income, and therefore may make you ineligible for public benefits.

Reverse Mortgage Safeguards

One of the best protections you have with reverse mortgages is the Federal Truth in Lending Act, which requires lenders to inform you about the plan's terms and costs. Be sure you understand them before signing.

COMPARING REVERSE MORTGAGES

When shopping for a reverse mortgage, keep this one key word in mind. CASH! How much total cash will you get, versus how much will you pay? Let me explain.

Savvy Shopping

Comparing one reverse mortgage to another, or to a Home Equity Conversion Mortgage, can be tricky. Your comparisons should weigh the total financial effect of one loan versus another. Here are a few tips to help you do that.

Home-Made Money

Reverse mortgages turn your home equity into three things:

- Loan advances paid to you
- Loan costs paid to the appraiser, lender, insurer, servicer and others
- Leftover equity, if any, paid to you or your heirs at the end of the loan

Three Questions

Because reverse mortgages turn home equity into three things, you can best analyze a reverse mortgage by asking three savvy questions:

- How much would I get?
- How much would I pay?
- How much would be left at the end of the loan?

☞ **SAVVY NOTE:** In comparing reverse mortgages, it is important to ask all three questions. You may prefer getting as much money as possible. But what if one loan paying you just a little more money has a much higher price tag? Or what if a plan paying the same money leaves you with a lot less equity?

Show Me the Money

To make comparisons, you must see where all of your home's value will go. At the end of a reverse mortgage, all of your home's value will have been turned into one of three things: loan advances, loan costs or leftover equity. Therefore, a key issue is how much of your home's value will go to you and your heirs versus how much of your home's value will be paid in loan costs to the lender, servicer, insurer and others. Remember, the bottom line is how much total cash you will get versus how much you will pay!

☞ **SAVVY NOTES:** FHA's reverse-mortgage insurance usually makes HUD's program less expensive to borrowers than the smaller reverse mortgage programs run by private lenders without FHA insurance.

HUD Service

Be sure to take advantage of your local HUD free housing-counseling service. You can get savvy housing advice on everything from reverse mortgages to buying a home, renting, defaults, foreclosures and credit issues. Call 1-800-569-4287 to locate the counseling agency nearest you, or visit *www.hud.gov*.

This information was obtained in part from the U.S. Department of Housing and Urban Development and AARP. You can receive free information about reverse mortgages by calling HUD at 1-800-209-8085.

SAVVY RESOURCES

- AARP: They offer a savvy free booklet, "Home-Made Money: A Consumer's Guide to Reverse Mortgages" (order #D15601). To order, call 1-800-424-3410 or log on at *www.aarp.org/revmort*.
- National Center for Home Equity Conversion: A nonprofit organization specializing in reverse-mortgage information; site includes news developments, a bibliography and a history of reverse mortgages. Visit *www.reverse.org*.
- National Reverse Mortgage Lenders Association: A trade group; site includes "best practices" for reverse-mortgage lenders, steps in getting a reverse mortgage, membership list. Visit *www.reversemortgage.org*.

— Long-Term-Care Insurance —

With the rising cost of nursing-home care today, many people are looking to long-term-care insurance as a way to protect their assets. Here is the short-term version on long-term care.

Long-term-care insurance helps pay for

- Care in a nursing home.
- Assisted-living services such as meals, health monitoring and help with daily activities, provided in a special residential setting other than your own home.
- Help in your home with daily activities such as bathing and dressing.
- Community programs such as adult day care.

 SAVVY NOTE: Long-term-care insurance is usually NOT covered by employer health insurance or Medicare or Medigap policies in any significant way (Medicare will pay for short-term skilled care). Medicaid does pay for long-term care, but you have to use most of your savings or other assets before you can receive benefits.

Nursing-Home Costs

Costs these days can range between—WOW—$30,000 and $90,000 per year, depending on the state you live in and the facility you go to. However, the national average cost is nearly $150 per day (almost $55,000 per year). Assisted living ranges anywhere from $50 to $100 per day.

When Should I Buy?

The older you are, the greater your chances of one day needing long-term-care services. Therefore, the older you are at the time you buy long-term-care insurance, the higher your premiums will be. If you buy when you are younger, premiums will be lower. However, you will be paying them for a longer period of time.

 SAVVY TIP: A recommended time to buy a policy is when you're between the ages of 55 and 60, before prices skyrocket and/or your health declines.

LONG-TERM CARE—IS IT FOR ME?

Some insurance salespersons will tell you that everybody needs long-term-care (LTC) insurance. NOT TRUE! When it comes to purchasing long-term-care insurance, remember that one size does not fit all. To help fit your needs, here are some savvy questions to ask yourself before you start shopping for a LTC policy:

- **What are my odds?** Some nursing-home statistics indicate an estimated 43 percent of Americans over age 65 are expected to spend some time in a nursing home during their lifetime. But you also need to know that the statistics also count the very short stays for which insurance may not be necessary. If you leave out nursing-home stays lasting less than three months, only about 33 percent of the population will spend time in a care facility.
- **Am I middle class?** Both wealthy and low-income patients probably don't need LTC insurance. Wealthy folks can afford nursing-home care on their own, and low-income people should be able to qualify for Medicaid. Middle-class-income earners are the best candidates for LTC insurance because they have assets to protect. Depending on where you live, people with assets ranging from $100,000 to less than $1.5 million would best benefit from LTC insurance.
- **Am I healthy?** In most cases it's disease that puts people in nursing homes, not old age! The diseases that cause the highest number of LTC insurance claims are Alzheimer's and other types of dementia followed by complications from strokes, fractures from falls and heart disease. What is your family history or risk for these?

 SAVVY FACT: The number of LTC policyholders in the United States has tripled, from 1.9 million in 1990 to 6.8 million in 1999.

Cost Considerations

If you were to decide to get LTC insurance, how much is enough? Long-term-care insurance policies vary greatly in what and how much they cover and in how much they charge. Here are some savvy questions to help you make policy decisions:

- **How long?** One potential way to keep your premiums from going high is to cap the length of your policy. Some policies will cover long-term care for three years, others for six, some for a lifetime.

 SAVVY NOTE: The lifetime LTC policy may not be necessary. The average claim length on long-term-care insurance policies is about two years.

- **How old?** The younger you are when you sign up, the less you'll pay for your premium. In 2003, an average policy (paying $150 per day for three years of coverage, with a 30-day waiting period and 5 percent compound inflation protection) cost a 50-year-old around $1,500 a year. The same policy cost a 60-year-old a little over $2,000 and a 70-year-old about $4,500.
- **How much?** Before you sign up, consider how much income you would have without insurance. Suppose nursing homes in your area cost $4,000 a month. If you have $3,000 per month of income coming in, you may need an insurance policy that covers the $1,000 difference.
- **Who's got a deal?** A common mistake is to automatically turn to your car or homeowners' insurance agent. LTC coverage is highly specialized, and you should check out a variety of companies before signing. Also remember to ask about spousal and family discounts. Some companies also give price breaks to very healthy individuals.

LTC insurance policies are complicated. It is savvy advice to have a qualified attorney or other person look over your contract before signing. This information was obtained in part from AARP and HIAA.

SAVVY RESOURCES

- Health Insurance Association of America (HIAA) offers a variety of useful LTC information: *www.hiaa.org*.
- National Association of Insurance Commissioners has a guide to shopping for long-term-care insurance: *www.naic.org*.

- Your local Area Agency on Aging can help you get information on comparing LTC policies. Call 1-800-677-1116.
- The Federal Long Term Care Insurance Program is available to federal and postal workers, government retirees and retired military personnel, as well as their immediate families. Call 1-800-582-3337 or visit *www.ltcfeds.com*.
- Long-Term Care Quote provides quotes on long-term-care policies. Visit *www.ltcq.net*.
- Insure.com compares the insurance rates of over 200 companies. Visit *www .insure.com*.

—Senior Debt—

The phrase "senior debt" used to conjure up images of college seniors graduating with loans they took out to pay for their education. Not so today, because the baby boomer population will begin retiring soon, and many of these people have lived with debt their entire lives.

Unsavvy Figures

Not long ago, CBS News reported that the amount of household debt for people over the age of 65 has tripled in the last decade. Keep in mind that these are not the boomers, so the entire problem can't be strapped to their backs.

Other figures indicate that nearly 60 percent of all seniors today carry some debt, compared to 35 percent a decade ago.

Bankruptcy courts also have seen a sharp increase in the number of seniors declaring bankruptcy. A Harvard study found that they are the fastest-growing group of bankruptcy filers. In 2001, the number of seniors declaring personal bankruptcy hit 82,000, up 244 percent from a decade earlier.

Times Have Changed

Many people used to see debt as a disease to be avoided, but the disease is not quite the killer it once was, when credit card companies were gouging people with rates of 20 and even 24 percent. Interest rates are at record lows, which means carrying debt is not the burden it once was, either; but it also means we should be paying off debt sooner. With good credit, people can refinance homes in the 5 percent range and even buy cars with next to no interest; however, that means seniors who rely on interest income are getting hammered. It's a classic Catch-22.

Pension plans of yesterday would in most cases give a guaranteed defined benefit. You knew where you stood and how much you needed to save to make ends meet in retirement. Today's 401(k)s, which many people now have, offer certain advantages, but they have one big drawback: People with them are relying on what are known as defined contribution plans, which don't guarantee a worker a set income at retirement. A bad choice or a bit of bad luck (like a big drop in the stock market), and they could lose a good portion of their retirement.

We all know what has happened to medical costs. They're climbing much faster than the rate of inflation, and putting seniors on fixed incomes in a tremendous bind. It's true that previous generations of retirees didn't have the level of debt that we do today, but health care wasn't as severe a burden back then, either.

SAVVY TIP: There are all the obvious things you can do, of course: Shop around for cheaper credit cards and refinance homes if you're still paying on them, for example. Counseling from a professional is a good idea for anyone contemplating retirement. But two things may ultimately be needed to reverse this societal trend: We're going to have to get medical costs under control, and more important, we have to learn to live within our means. Which means changing our lifestyles, which is a much tougher trick.

SAVVY RESOURCES

- CardWeb.com, Inc.: Offers a comprehensive guide to low-interest, no-fee and secured credit cards. Call 1-800-344-7714 or visit *www.cardweb.com*.

- National Foundation for Consumer Credit Counseling: Offers free or low-cost counseling that is very useful. Call 1-800-388-2227 or visit *www.nfcc.org*.
- National Association of Consumer Advocates NACA: a nonprofit association of attorneys and consumer advocates committed to representing customers' interests. Call 1-202-452-1989 or visit *www.naca.net*.
- National Consumer Law Center: *www.consumerlaw.org*.

MEDICAL DEBT

The National Consumer Law Center reports that one out of every seven older Americans has found it very difficult to pay medical bills, and many have seen it eat up their savings, even with health insurance. Many seniors have five-, six- and even seven-figure debt from prolonged hospital stays. And hospitals are getting tougher and more aggressive with those who can't or won't pay.

Now, I'm not advocating not paying the bill. That's not fair to the medical community or to other patients who will absorb the costs, and it could come back to bite you if you need more medical care in the future. But the first trick in any tight spot is finding out your options.

- **Negotiate:** The National Consumer Law Center recommends negotiating with the hospital. And not just the amount you'll pay each month, either, but negotiate the size of the bill. Review it thoroughly. Find out what they are charging for some of the basic services and watch out for $10 aspirins and $25 Band-Aids. And if there is something outrageous in there, such as that $100 bedpan, let the hospital know you'll call a newspaper. Keep in mind that insurance companies negotiate bills all the time: In fact, in order to give HMOs some of those deep discounts, they shift their costs to third-party payers. I know of a man who recently received a $16,000 bill following a surgery, but the hospital settled with the HMO for $4,000. All the patient paid was his deductible. Find out if this cost-shifting is a game your hospital is playing. If so, work with your insurance provider to leverage a discount.

- **Financial Planning:** The next step is for you to set your priorities. Determine exactly which are your most important bills, such as the house payment, the groceries and ongoing prescriptions. But if you drop your medical payments down the ladder, realize that doing so can affect your ability to receive future medical care. See a financial planner or credit counselor to help you set up a good payment plan.
- **Bankruptcy:** A third and more painful option is, of course, bankruptcy. This once had a stigma associated with it, but some studies, such as one printed in the *New York University Law Review,* found that overwhelming medical debt is responsible for up to 45 percent of all bankruptcies. But you want to do this in such a way that you protect your home and other assets as much as possible.

Bankruptcy Basics

There are two primary types of personal bankruptcy: Chapter 13 and Chapter 7. Each must be filed in federal bankruptcy court. The current fees for seeking bankruptcy relief are $160: a filing fee of $130 and an administrative fee of $30. Attorney fees are additional and can vary widely.

- Chapter 13 allows you, if you have a regular income and limited debt, to keep property, such as a mortgaged house or car, that you otherwise might lose. In Chapter 13, the court approves a repayment plan that allows you to pay off a default during a period of three to five years, rather than surrender any property.
- Chapter 7, known as straight bankruptcy, involves liquidating all assets that are not exempt. Exempt property may include cars, work-related tools and basic household furnishings. Some property may be sold by a court-appointed official (a trustee) or turned over to creditors. You can receive a discharge of your debts under Chapter 7 only once every six years.

Both types of bankruptcy may get rid of unsecured debts and stop foreclosures, re-possessions, garnishments, utility shut-offs and debt-collection activities. Both also provide exemptions that allow you to keep certain assets, although exemption amounts vary. Personal bankruptcy usually does not erase child support, alimony, fines, taxes and some student-loan obligations. Also, unless you have an acceptable plan to catch up on your debt under Chapter 13, bankruptcy usually does not allow you to keep property when your creditor has an unpaid mortgage or lien on it.

 SAVVY TIP: Get familiar with your rights regarding debt collection. Most state governments have fair-credit debt collection statutes that are aimed at stopping deceptive collection tactics, preventing harassment and limiting the ways in which a credit agency can contact you. Call your state or county consumer protection offices, or your county attorney or state attorney general's office for help.

Second Mortgage Note: Don't—I repeat—don't take out a second mortgage on your home to pay for medical costs. If you do this, you'll be converting unsecured debt into secured debt. Let me explain: Since you already have received the medical care, the hospital can't take it away from you; but if you put your house on the line with a second mortgage and then fail to make those payments, you could lose your house. Suddenly, your unfortunate situation will have grown into a disaster.

SAVVY NOTE: The only scenario for taking out that second mortgage for medical care is for upfront costs, such as the need to raise $50,000 for a heart transplant in advance of the surgery.

SAVVY RESOURCES

- The Patient Advocate Foundation: a national nonprofit organization that can help you sort out your bills for free if you've got a chronic, life-threatening or debilitating disease. Visit *www.patientadvocate.org.*
- Healthcare Ombudsman Office: Offered in many states, they support and promote programs that help people with health-insurance problems. Visit *www.healthassistancepartnership.org* (click on "Program Locator").